D0207272

The Cultural World of Jesus

The Cultural World of Jesus
Sunday by Sunday
Cycle A

John J. Pilch

A Liturgical Press Book

 THE LITURGICAL PRESS
Collegeville, Minnesota

12   13   14   15   16

Library of Congress Cataloging-in-Publication Data

Pilch, John J.
    The cultural world of Jesus : Sunday by Sunday / John J. Pilch.
        p. cm.
    Includes bibliographical references.
    Contents: [1] Cycle A
    ISBN 0-8146-2286-0 (cycle A)
    1. Bible N. T. Gospels–Liturgical lessons, English. 2. Bible. N. T. Gospels–Meditations. 3. Bible. N. T. Gospels–History of Biblical events. 4. Middle East–Civilization. I. Title.
BX2170.C55P49   1995
264'.34–dc20   94-44772
                                                          CIP

For Bruce J. Malina,
friend, colleague, and inspiration,
a true lover of the Word.

Contents

Introduction

The idea for these reflections from a Mediterranean cultural perspective on the Gospel read at Sunday liturgies originated in a monthly column I wrote for *Modern Liturgy* between 1989 and 1991. When my tenure as columnist ended, I persuaded my agents, Initiatives Etc., of Columbus, Ohio, to publish a brief weekly reflection on a subscription basis.

This one-page bulletin-insert quickly became very popular with adult enrichment and RCIA groups. I have been delighted when visiting parishes to conduct Bible study seminars to see parishioners diligently reading the insert and checking the missalette before Mass.

It has been even more satisfying to hear the preacher say: "My topic this morning is x. Other interesting ideas about today's Gospel can be found in the bulletin insert. I encourage you to read and reflect on that page with your Bible at home. For this morning, however, let us reflect on my topic, x." Often the preacher further develops a topic from the insert and makes significantly appropriate applications to the local community.

This collection of reflections is revised and slightly larger than the subscription series. The architects of the Lectionary have provided readings for fifty-six Sundays in each year's Cycle. No liturgical year lasts fifty-six weeks. Lent, Easter, and other feasts cause various Sundays to be omitted each year. This collection treats only the Gospels assigned for the fifty-six Sundays as found in the Lectionary. It does not include the Gospels for feasts that sometimes fall on a Sunday.

The Interpretation of the Bible in the Church, published in 1993 by the Pontifical Biblical Commission, highlighted some distinctive insights that Mediterranean cultural anthropology can shed on interpreting the Bible. The concepts enumerated in these paragraphs reflect the publications of The Context Group, an association of biblical scholars of which I am a charter member. For nearly two decades this group has dedicated itself to studying the Mediterranean backgrounds of the New Testament. The Biblical Commission's document represents concepts developed in research papers read by Context Group members at a scientific meeting in Spain in 1991. The list of recommended readings that concludes this volume reports these ground-breaking studies whose insights are liberally reflected in my reflections.

I have not listed the excellent Gospel commentaries and commentaries on the Lectionary that adopt other approaches and are readily available for anyone desiring a more comprehensive treatment of these texts. The focus here is almost exclusively on the Mediterranean cultural perspective.

Purists or sensates on the Myers-Briggs scale may object to the global adjective "Mediterranean." They will correctly insist on recognizing the differences of each country in this part of the world. Nevertheless, reputable specialists in Mediterranean culture convincingly demonstrate that this region (which they sometimes call "Circum-Mediterranean"— see George Foster, *Culture and Conquest* [Chicago: Quadrangle Books, 1960] 25) share many cultural elements unchanged over several millennia. The core values of honor and shame are two such basic elements. Details of honorable and shameful behavior do indeed differ from country to country. These reflections present the characteristics of the first-century eastern Mediterranean region.

Thus, I use the words "Mediterranean" or "Middle Eastern" precisely to describe the culture of the people who populate, and whose lives are reflected in, the Bible. The insights about the culture of this world are derived from contemporary anthropological investigations, particularly the research of Mediterranean anthropologists such as Lila Abu-Lughod, Camillia Fawzi El-Solh, Soraya Altorki, Elizabeth Warnock Fernea, David Gilmore, and members of The Context Group.

Anthropologists agree that the judicious use of contemporary data, linked to historical accounts, is basic and reliable anthropological methodology (see Foster, *Culture and Conquest*, 30). It is legitimate anthropological method to retroject contemporary insights over two and three thousand years because, until the advent of colonialism and the discovery of oil and its consequences, the culture of the region remained remarkably unchanged.

In sum, these reflections are an attempt to fulfill the exhortations of the Second Vatican Council, which urged interpreters of the Bible to pay due attention to "the characteristic styles of perceiving" that prevailed at the time of the sacred author (On Revelation, no. 12). Perception is governed by culture. The better an interpreter knows the culture in which the Bible originated, the more culturally plausible will be the interpretation.

It is exactly this understanding that stands behind the instruction for preachers that cautions: "When they narrate biblical events, let them not add imaginative details which are not consonant with the truth" (The 1964 Instruction on the Historical Truth of the Gospels, par. XIII). The phrase "consonant with the truth" is best rendered "culturally plausible."

Moreover, *The Interpretation of the Bible in the Church* urges preachers to focus on the central contribution of Lectionary texts in order to actualize and inculturate the text appropriately in the lives of the listeners. The approach of cultural anthropology that characterizes the reflections in this book is admirably suited to helping achieve this goal in the liturgy.

Preachers are fond of quoting the literal Greek translation from John's Gospel, that Jesus "became human and pitched his tent among us" (1:14). Specifically and in the concrete, Jesus was a first-century, Middle-Eastern peasant, driven by the core cultural values of honor and shame, expert in the art of challenge and riposte, and master of all his culture's strategies. The challenge to Western believers is to understand and appreciate Jesus on his own terms. To this I hope my reflections make some modest contribution.

Feast of St. Bonaventure   John J. Pilch
July 14, 1994   Georgetown University

First Sunday of Advent
Matthew 24:37-44

What American does not think about or prepare for the future? Americans save for a rainy day, to get married, to buy a home, to send the children to college, and to retire in comfort. Americans also protect themselves against future misfortunes with varieties of insurance.

Jesus' advice to his contemporaries, "Stay awake!" and be prepared for an imminent event, belabors the obvious for Americans (vv. 42-43). However, future events are not obvious for Middle Easterners.

PRESENT FOCUS

Generally speaking, people in the Middle East are unable and unwilling to think about the future. Only God knows that, and it is futile for humans to try to discover it. Daniel's revised calculations of a coming event (1290 days; 1335 days; forget it!; see Dan 12:11-13) are humorous to the modern reader, but they illustrate well the viewpoint of our Middle Eastern ancestors.

People of that world live entirely for the present. Jesus chides them for worrying about tomorrow and what they will eat, drink, or wear (Matt 6:25-34). He instructs them to ask God only for today's bread and not a week's supply (Matt 6:11).

Jesus is absolutely convinced that "this [that is, his own, first-century] generation will not pass away until all these things have taken place" (Matt 24:34).

Where, then, did today's exhortation to "stay awake" and "be watchful" for the "advent of the Son of Man" come from? Did Jesus say these words, or were they placed on his lips by his disciples?

PRESENT FRUSTRATION

Scholars point out that Jesus frequently proposed behaviors alternative to those favored in his culture. Obsessive and narrow focus on the present can cause a person to miss events just around the corner (which are also present but slightly delayed).

By the time Matthew compiled his Gospel, around 80 to 85 C.E., Jesus had been dead and risen nearly fifty years. About ten to fifteen years prior to Matthew's work, the failed revolt of the Judeans resulted in the utter demolition of their Temple by Titus and his Roman legions (70 C.E.).

Still, the Son of Man had not yet returned, and many of Jesus' original listeners had already died. Christians were frightened and becoming impatient.

Matthew's community was further agitated by its vocal Judean opponents. Their taunt to the Christians ran something like this: "Where is your 'coming Son of Man?' You keep saying 'in *this* generation,' but you are deceived. Remember Daniel's inability to calculate and predict? You are similarly misguided. Give it up!"

HOPE FOR THE "FUTURE"

For today's reading, Matthew has borrowed and redirected parables from Mark 13 to console and instruct his beleaguered community. The Son of Man gave his word; he definitely will return (v. 35).

No one can calculate the exact time because his coming will be unexpected, just as the flood was for Noah's contemporaries (vv. 37-39). For this reason, the Christian must be ever watchful. The parables about the two in the field (v. 40) and two grinding (v. 41) give no clue as to which will be taken and which will remain. Each person must be vigilant like the good homeowner, wary of thieves and vandals (v. 43). Each must be ever prepared for the Lord's sudden return.

For our present-oriented ancestors in the faith, the ongoing delay of Jesus' expected imminent return forced them to think "future." When this delay had reached fifty years and more in Matthew's community, the evangelist was able to force his present-oriented people to begin to think of at least a slightly remote, if not yet very far off, future.

The challenge to American believers is quite different. Americans are so terminally future oriented, often to a distant future (college for the infant; retirement for the new worker), that they frequently miss the present entirely.

The digital watch with no second hand and the computer that operates in milli- and nano-seconds reinforce our sense of a fleeting, practically non-existent present moment. With our futures relatively well-secured, we need to be wakeful to and watchful of the present lest misfortune creep up on us before we realize it.

Second Sunday of Advent
Matthew 3:1-12

JOHN THE DIPPER

The word *baptism*, which is transliterated directly from the Greek, actually means "dipping in a liquid." In Mediterranean antiquity, water, fire, and wind (or spirit) were viewed as liquids that could be poured upon or into people.

John performed his dipping in the shallow waters of the Jordan, quite likely after the rainy season (late September to late April) when the water would be warmer. Jewish ritual purity baths were not heated except for the extremely wealthy few (less than 2 percent of city population).

JOHN'S AUDIENCE

"Groups" came to John (from Jerusalem, all Judea, the Jordan region, v. 5) because in antiquity only group travel was safe. Ideal travel was with kin and fictive kin.

Moreover, travel in antiquity was considered deviant behavior unless one had a specific reason like pilgrimage or coming out to hear a prophet.

Of course John summoned individuals to repentance, but he lumped them into groups, as we shall see.

JOHN'S PURPOSE

By word and symbol, John preaches repentance, particularly group repentance, namely, the reform of Israel (see v. 2). John's garb (camel's-hair clothing cinched with a leather

4

belt) and food (locusts and honey) symbolically link him with Samson, Samuel, and Elijah, who represent the Old Testament tradition of resistance to injustice and the revolutionary model of renewing society.

John's preaching challenges various groups to reform. Clearly the prophet and his sympathetic listeners are dissatisfied with the status quo. In the life of Jesus, the transfiguration and resurrection should also be viewed as symbols of transformation calling for conversion, repentance, reform, social change, revolution, and radical transformation of the human condition.

NAME CALLING

At a very obvious level, John challenges elites to reform their lives. The basic claim to honor in a society whose core values are honor and shame is made through birth. One is born into an honorable status, whatever it may be. Imagine the impact of John the Dipper publicly and loudly calling the "honorable" Pharisees and Sadducees "snake-bastards"! The phrase "brood of vipers" attributes their paternity to snakes rather than humans and directly challenges their basic claim to honor!

Anticipating a counter-argument from the crowd, John goes on to challenge the biological basis of honor in general ("Abraham is our father") and urges a moral basis instead ("bear good fruit"). Not who one is but what one does should be paramount.

DIVIDED SOCIETY

On a less obvious level, John challenges the priestly aristocracy. While many have thought that Judean society in first-century Palestine was divided between priests versus people as a whole, the division was actually more between high priesthood (the Jerusalem elite) and the people and their ordinary priests (like Zechariah, the father of John) living in the outlying villages.

The oppression worked upon the people and their ordinary priests by the Jerusalem elite and their Roman patrons was experienced in exorbitant taxes, confiscation of ancestral property, and chronic shortages of food, among other things. This contributed much to social unrest and desire for change. John's priestly descent from an ordinary priest gave him firsthand experience of the problem. It very likely inspired and shaped his prophetic preaching.

FINAL WORD

John the Dipper concluded his preaching with a play on the symbolism of liquids (water, fire, wind-spirit). His symbolic dipping of repentant Israelites in warm water will be replaced with a judgmental dipping by "him who is to come" in the liquid of "holy wind or spirit" and fire. Now is the time for listeners to repent and escape the judgment.

For modern American believers, Advent often means commemorating the birth of the baby Jesus and preparing to celebrate Christmas in the grand tradition of charity to the needy and gift giving. The intensely political coloring of the Baptist's activity should give modern believers pause. Have we diluted his challenge?

Third Sunday of Advent
Matthew 11:2-11

Here Matthew presents the contrasting opinions of John the Baptist and Jesus about each other. John is confused about Jesus' identity, but Jesus is very certain about John's identity and status.

WHO IS JESUS?

John's question is clear: Is Jesus the "one who is to come" or not? Its meaning is far from clear. In Jesus' time there was no uniform or even dominant Judean idea about the Messiah. There wasn't even a uniform understanding of Judaism. The multiplicity of ideas in this period prompts contemporary scholars to talk about "Judaisms" and "their Messiahs."

Jesus' answer is equally ambiguous. If he is thinking of Isaiah 35:5-6, his list of credentials could be interpreted as powerful deeds a messiah might do. If instead he is thinking of the *Psalms of Solomon* 17 (a first-century B.C.E. composition), then he has in mind the ideal Jewish king who is primarily a military and political leader. The safest opinion is that Jesus accepts the designation "one who is to come" whatever it means.

JESUS' CREDENTIALS

Professional healers in Jesus' time preferred to talk about illnesses rather than heal them. A physician who failed to heal a sick person risked being put to death for lack of success. Such physicians are rarely mentioned in the New Testament (see Mark 5:26) and then mainly in sarcastic proverbs commonly repeated in Mediterranean literature (see Luke 4:23).

Among the peasants, however, folk healers willing to use their hands and risk failure were very common (Matt 17:14-16). Jesus was one of these. Small wonder that Jesus reminds the imprisoned and confused Baptist about his successes as a prophet-healer (Matt 11:5).

Isn't Jesus boasting and thereby violating the honor rules of his culture? Isn't a Mediterranean person obliged to deny compliments (Matt 20:29-31) and avoid the appearance of grasping for honor (Matt 10:24-25) in order not to impinge on someone else's honor? Jesus anticipates the charge and protects himself against it by concluding with a "beatitude": "Truly honorable and esteemed is the one who takes no offense at my rightful claim to honor!" (v. 6).

WHO IS JOHN?

Jesus asks: "What did you go out to see: John, or the grass/reed?" The Greek word describes a "reed" that grew only in Egypt and from which pens were made. There is no doubt, however, that the evangelists are referring to the tall and graceful *Arundo donax* which grows abundantly and luxuriously along the streams in the Jordan valley. Its light and feathery head is sensitive to the slightest breeze (1 Kgs 14:15). Its straight and strong stem was used as a walking stick (2 Kgs 18:21), measuring rod (Ezek 40:3), and other useful items. Possibly Jesus intended to contrast the unbending convictions of John with the resilient and flexible grass.

Jesus' second probing question, contrasting John's rough Elijah-like clothing with soft garments, may be an intentional comparison of the prophet with the weak-willed Herod Antipas who would put John to death in a short while (14:1-12).

Today's reading concludes with Jesus' affirmation that John is more than a prophet (v. 9) and his honor rating (based on his birth, v. 11) is unsurpassed. But, Jesus adds, the least in the reign of heaven has a higher honor rating than John (v. 12).

At this point, Matthew's Jesus leaves matters up in the air. Is John part of the reign of God, or excluded from it? Jesus ends with the ultimate ambiguity: "If you are willing to accept it, John is Elijah who is to come" (v. 14). There is no evidence that in the first century C.E. it was widely known or commonly accepted that Elijah is a forerunner of the Messiah. Such an idea seems to be a Christian adaptation of Malachi 4:5-6 put on Jesus' lips long after he died.

Confused? Americans may recall Senator Howard Baker's persistent question in the Watergate hearings: "What did the President [Nixon] know, and when did he know it?" Today's reflection on this gospel selection demonstrates that Scripture does not easily yield a satisfying answer to such a question. That should be no surprise. We are Christians, after all, by faith, and not by force of irrefutable evidence.

Fourth Sunday of Advent
Matthew 1:18-24

The circumstances of Jesus' conception and birth described by Matthew take on sharper contours when viewed in their Mediterranean cultural context.

BETROTHAL AND MARRIAGE

It would be wrong to consider betrothal as similar to our idea of engagement before marriage. Betrothal was the initial phase of the marriage process in which prospective spouses (commonly first cousins, see Gen 24:4; 28:20) were set apart for each other. Though a betrothed couple did not live together, a formal divorce was required to break the public establishment of the betrothal. Sex with a betrothed woman was considered adultery (Deut 22:23-24).

In the ancient Mediterranean world, marriages were arranged by parents to join extended families and not individuals. The bride did not expect love, companionship, or comfort. In this rigidly gender-divided world, men and women had very little contact. Both partners realized that their union was arranged for the political or economic advantage of their families.

The entire marriage process is a ritualized removal of a woman from her family. The groom's father offers gifts or services to the bride's father to win the wife he wants for his son. The bride's father makes the final decision. The women of both families negotiate the contract to be certain neither family is shortchanged, but the patriarch of each family ratifies the contract publicly. When the groom takes the bride into his home, the marriage process is completed (see Matt 25:1-12 and the commentary on the Thirty-Second Sunday in Ordinary Time).

MARY'S PREGNANCY

Given the very nosey nature of Mediterranean village life, the separation of men from women, and the fact that the betrothed couple were not yet living together, Joseph may have been among the last to learn of Mary's pregnancy. Women would have noticed that she was not participating in their obligatory monthly ritual purification.

Matthew inserts an explanation for his readers: Mary is pregnant by a spirit that is holy. Joseph will have to learn this in another way.

JOSEPH'S PREDICAMENT

The honor code of the Mediterranean world demands that no one take what properly belongs to another. Mary's child is not Joseph's, so he hesitates to take it. He also knows that he will be unable to display publicly the "tokens of virginity" (Deut 22:13-21) on his wedding night. If he doesn't act quickly, he will be shamed.

By law, Joseph is entitled to return Mary to her father and expose her to death. Numbers 5:11-31 describes the ordeal Mary would have to undergo. But Joseph is an honorable man and determines to divorce her leniently. His sense of honor hopes that the rightful father will seize this opportunity to claim the child and marry Mary. In all of his decision, Joseph acts very honorably.

THE WILL OF GOD

Our Mediterranean ancestors in the faith generally tried to live by the will of God. But how did God make his will known and how did people learn it? The elites such as Herod resorted to the very expensive option of consulting Scripture experts (see Matt 2:5-6).

Ordinary folk had to rely on ordinary means. The prophet Joel (2:28) reports a proverb that captures a basic Mediterranean belief: "Old men dream dreams, young men see visions." That Joseph (Matt 1:20-21; 2:13, 19) and the astrologers (2:12) learn God's will in a dream is not only the ordinary way of learning God's will but also an allusion to their age. (Yet remember that less than 5 percent of the population lived to the age of thirty!)

God personally announces to Joseph the gender of the child (a highly prized male is a special gift of God in this culture) and assigns his name (Jesus). This fact immediately immerses Jesus in honor far surpassing human calculation and further enhances Joseph's honorable reputation, for God would not honor a shameful person.

In an effort to contemporize the biblical record, some modern preachers speak of Mary as a pregnant, unwed, teenage girl and describe Jesus' family as homeless. These clever descriptions are ill-suited to Mediterranean culture and are unfair to Mary, Joseph, and Jesus. While the circumstances and embarrassment of Mary's predicament look similar to American experiences, the consequences in her culture are radically different.

Holy Family
Matthew 2:13-15, 19-23

Throughout his Gospel, Matthew presents Jesus as another Moses. This emphasis begins already in Matthew 2, from which today's reading is drawn.

MOSES

The basic story line in Exodus describes the wicked Pharaoh who decrees that Moses and all male Hebrew children should be murdered (1:16, 22). Pharaoh's daughter manages to save Moses (2:1-10). As a young man, Moses kills an Egyptian and has to flee for his life to Midian (2:15). After Pharaoh dies, the Lord commands Moses to return from Midian to Egypt (4:19).

In the first century, it was popular to retell and embellish the Moses story rather freely. The versions in Josephus (*Antiquities* 2.205–37) and pseudo-Philo (9.9–15) are two excellent examples of this kind of rewritten Bible which have parallels in Matthew 2. The evangelist wants his readers to see a continuity between Moses and Jesus.

HEROD

Because of a miscalculation in the sixth century by the monk Dionysius Exiguus, who arranged the calendar we follow to this day, Jesus was actually born about 6 B.C.E. and Herod died about 4 B.C.E. Herod was a ruthless king who didn't hesitate to kill family members to preserve his position. Joseph learns of Herod's intrigue and God's will to save the child in a dream instructing him to flee with his family to Egypt.

Egypt was a traditional place of refuge for Judeans (see 1 Kgs 11:20; Jer 26:21). It came under Roman rule in 30 B.C.E. and was beyond Herod's jurisdiction.

HEROD'S SONS

Herod had three sons: Archelaus, Herod Antipas, and Philip. He sent them as young men to Rome to learn how to be rulers. When Herod died, Archelaus inherited Judea, Samaria, and Idumaea. He was every bit as cruel a ruler as his father.

Herod Antipas received Galilee and Perea. This is the Herod who beheaded John and whom Jesus called "that fox." Galilee was much more peaceful and a little more secure than Judea. This might explain why Joseph elected to settle the family there instead of in Bethlehem.

NAZARETH OF GALILEE

Though Matthew calls Nazareth a city, it was a hamlet numbering about a hundred people. There were a few families at most, very likely all related to each other. In such a village, first-cousin marriage partners would be easy to find.

This hamlet was not far from the sea highway, the principal trade route to and from Egypt. Another major road from Acco toward Tiberias crossed the sea highway near Nazareth. Located so close to a major crossroads, Nazareth understandably gravitated toward the "big" city of Sepphoris at that crossroads.

Mentioned nowhere in the Bible, Sepphoris was very important. In Jesus' time it was the district capitol where Herod Antipas carried out massive building programs providing work for artisans in the region. Around the year 200 C.E. Rabbi Judah the Prince spent the last years of his life there codifying the Mishna. Galilee thus was the birthplace of both Christianity and post-biblical talmudic Judaism.

THE HOLY FAMILY

Modern Americans who imagine Jesus, Mary, and Joseph as a nuclear family inappropriately transform them into Americans. The Middle Eastern family is enormous and quite extended. It is highly probable that they had relatives in Bethlehem and that all the inhabitants of Nazareth were members of Jesus' extended family. Middle Eastern families relate differently, too. The strongest emotional bond is between mother and oldest son. It remains so throughout their lives. The weakest emotional bond is between husband and wife.

Though we know precious little about this family's life in Nazareth after returning from Egypt, Matthew portrays Jesus as quite capable of functioning effectively in the public world of the male. His large, extended family raised him well.

Finally, note Matthew's combination of place-names with Scripture quotations. The flight into Egypt is related to Hosea 11:1, and the return to Nazareth is said to have a basis in Scripture (still unidentified). This suggests that Jesus' family directed him toward his destiny "according to the Scriptures," that is, in harmony with God's will as revealed in the Bible. Oh that this might be true for contemporary families as well!

Epiphany
Matthew 2:1-12

Since all people are born more or less equal, ancient biographers like Plutarch regularly "created" special origins and extraordinary circumstances for the great people whose lives they narrated. Though it is a very complicated issue, scholars agree that Matthew has similarly embellished and probably created stories about the birth of Jesus who was put to death presumably for claiming to be "king of the Judeans" (Matt 27:37). This story of the Magi illustrates the plausible mixture of fact with literary creativity.

MAGI IN THE EAST

The Greek word *magoi* in this story has been translated in modern times as "wise men" (too generic), "kings" (incorrect), and "astrologers" (partially correct but confusing because of modern connotations). The revised New Testament of the New American Bible restores the word "Magi."

In the cultural world of Jesus, Magi were a caste of very high ranking political-religious advisers to the rulers of the Median and then the Persian empires (roughly equivalent to the modern countries of Iran and Iraq).

The ancient writers Strabo and Xenophon point out that in Persia Magi communicated with the high god Ahura Mazdah on behalf of the Great King, or as they called him, the King of Kings. The fact that at one point Magi successfully revolted against and replaced the king indicates that they were also an ever-present internal threat for Persia.

History notes that Magi also resisted the imperialistic designs of Philip the Macedonian and Alexander the Great to conquer the ancient Near Eastern people. The Greeks viewed the Persians as decadent and weak. The Persians obviously resented that. Indeed, Persian prophecies similar to Daniel's vision of four kingdoms each more decadent than the preceding (Babylonian, Median, Persian, Hellenistic) yearned for a restoration of true Persian kingship.

When the Romans began to dominate the world scene, the Magi increased their support for Eastern (Persian) kingship and encouraged resistance against Western (Roman) imperialism. In 66 C.E., while putting down the Judean revolt in Jerusalem, the Romans agreed to accept the Parthian candidate Tiridates as legitimate king of Armenia rather than appoint a puppet king like Herod and his sons in Israel. Tiridates took the sons of three neighboring Parthian rulers and an entourage including Magi, relatives, servants, three thousand horsemen and numerous Romans, and made an expenses-paid (by the Romans), nine-month pilgrimage to "bend the knee" to and accept the crown from Nero at Rome.

This historical event was burned into the memories of everyone in the first-century Mediterranean world. Clearly the Magi had enormous influence as advisers to Eastern kings. Matthew was undoubtedly familiar with the story.

MATTHEW'S MAGI

In the hypothetically recreated "original" story of the Magi and Jesus, the Magi chart Jesus' horoscope, discover and follow his star, find and worship him, and leave. How does Matthew reshape this event to fit into the birth story of Jesus?

Drawing inspiration from the Tiridates story, Matthew puts a very appropriate political spin on Jesus' story. Known for their centuries-old opposition to Western (currently Roman) imperialism, the Eastern Magi travel to submit to Jesus, a new "king of Judeans."

The Magi proclaim a message that resounds beyond the confines of Israel to the entire ancient Near East. Here in this babe is the new King of Kings. Here begins the restoration of true Eastern kingship. That Roman bootlicking, murderous, and tyrannical puppet-king, Herod the Great, has every reason to squirm.

To add insult to Herod's injury, the gospel story interprets the visit of the Magi as saying that liberation from foreign domination and restored Eastern kingship has come not from the elite but rather from the poor and humble in a hamlet (Bethlehem) of a rather insignificant principality (Judea).

Christian tradition and liturgy have overlaid the visit of the Magi, Jesus' "epiphany," with engaging symbolism and rich interpretations. We do well to remember that at the heart of this story as in all the stories of the Bible lies plain history, real politics, and human effort viewed through an ever-changing assortment of lenses.

Baptism of the Lord
Matthew 3:13-17

One of the most certain historical facts recorded in the Gospels is that John baptized Jesus. Each Gospel, however, presents a different significance or interpretation of this fact.

SEASONS

In first-century Israel there were two seasons: rainy (from late September to late April) and dry (early May to early September). During the rainy season people stayed indoors. During the dry season, people could be out and about, a very important Mediterranean activity. People there love to see and be seen. In this regard, Jesus and his disciples were typical Mediterraneans.

That Jesus and others could be "dipped" in the Jordan indicates it was the beginning of the dry season, when the Jordan and its streams would have been filled with the winter rains and the sun had warmed the shallow waters to a comfortable temperature.

In Matthew's Gospel Jesus' ministry lasts one dry season. He dies at Passover, a harvest feast celebrated at the beginning of the next dry season. In John's Gospel, Jesus' ministry covers a period of three dry seasons because he makes three trips to Jerusalem to observe the springtime feast of Passover.

JESUS' IDENTITY

In Matthew, the voice from heaven announces: "This is my beloved Son with whom I am well pleased." Hasn't the evangelist already made this point in the first two chapters of his Gospel? Remember that in this honor-driven society, one must establish that value at every opportunity. Matthew's genealogy for Jesus (different from Luke's) puts him in the honorable lineage of Abraham and David. At his conception, Jesus had honorable spiritual origins. His obedient mother and just father are equally honorable. Matthew's entire Gospel demonstrates Jesus' continuity with Moses, his honorable ancestor.

In the baptism, a public event witnessed by everyone present, God personally proclaims a relationship of father and son, patron and client, with Jesus. Without this public declaration, Jesus would have been unable to initiate his ministry. Even so, Jesus' hometown neighbors remained skeptical: "Is this not the carpenter's son? . . . Where did he get all of this?" (Matt 13:54-58).

SIGNIFICANCE OF THE DIPPING

From the earliest times, the followers of Jesus were embarrassed by his submission to John's baptism. John, after all, explained that his baptism was for the purpose of repentance (Matt 3:11). Being superior to John (Matt 3:11-12), Jesus did not need to repent.

Matthew's account offers two explanations to ease the embarrassment. One is common to all three accounts of Jesus' baptism, namely, the voice from heaven. In the Hebrew Scripture, this voice is called the "daughter of the voice" *(bat qol),* that is, the "echo" of something God has spoken.

The Aramaic paraphrases of the Old Testament, called "Targums," frequently feature a "voice from heaven" that explains questionable events like Abraham's attempt to murder his son Isaac (Gen 22:10), or why the angels in Jacob's dream (Gen 28:12) are descending instead of ascending as is traditional. The voice from heaven in Matthew says that Jesus is baptized because God wills it. God is pleased by Jesus' obedience, which in turn suggests that Jesus deserves obedience from his followers.

The second explanation which is peculiar to Matthew's Gospel is Jesus' claim that he must "fulfill all righteousness."

Scholars understand this to mean that, like many people, Jesus was intrigued by John's reputation and went out to see him. Then John's exhortation to repentance caused a change of heart in him, a conversion.

Jesus was an artisan. While there is no evidence to indicate that he ever cheated clients, he recognized the risks entailed in his profession and accepted John's call to "produce good fruits." Jesus was baptized in order to please God. As a result, he became John's disciple and shared in the dipping ministry. (See John 3:22 which reports Jesus' baptizing ministry, and contrast John 4:1-2, the later Christian tradition, which denies it.)

How refreshing for American believers to realize that Jesus, too, had to discover his identity, discern God's will for him, and pursue his destiny. Jesus' beliefs helped him. How do our beliefs help us?

Second Sunday in Ordinary Time
John 1:29-34

While the evangelist John has a deserved reputation as a theological and mystical author, he also presents some sobering glimpses into "real history."

In today's reading, we learn that John the Baptizer was not very familiar with his kinsman, Jesus, and had difficulty recognizing him (vv. 30, 33). In spite of this, the Baptizer proclaims himself a "witness" to Jesus.

A MEDITERRANEAN "WITNESS"

A colleague of mine recently spent his sabbatical with the family of a friend in Naples. The friend asked my colleague to serve as a witness in a lawsuit to stop a neighbor from physically abusing the friend's son.

My colleague went to the attorney, who asked, "What did you see?" My colleague said: "I did not witness the fights. But in my apartment I could hear the noises in the street, later I saw the bruised boy with tattered clothing. Moreover, I have seen the boy come home from school frequently in such shape, and he reports that the neighbor is beating him up."

The attorney's face blanched. He sat back in his chair and said: "That's all you saw? This makes me want to quit practicing law. Never in my career have I met such an honest witness."

My colleague learned that "to see" in that cultural context means to report what one feels, imagines, presumes, or desires, especially if it will help a friend in need. He should have described in great detail with strong emotion the beatings he never saw. This is what that culture expects of a "witness."

JOHN THE WITNESS

The people who populate the pages of our New Testament are from that same general region of the world as my colleague's friend. We can expect them to "testify" in similar fashion.

Trials in ancient Israel were decided by the leading men of the city or synagogue who administered justice "in the gate" (see Amos 5:15; Deut 19:12). They did not investigate facts but rather made a decision on the admissibility and competence of witnesses who spoke either in defense of or against an accused person. The person who could muster the most impressive array of witnesses usually won.

John's Gospel in general has a strong forensic character. Chief among the impressive witnesses is John the Baptizer. Speaking to his opponents, Jesus says of John: "He was a burning and shining lamp, and you were willing to rejoice for a while in his light" (John 5:32-35). Other important witnesses in John's Gospel are Jesus' works, God, and Scripture.

Jesus' enemies in this Gospel frequently consulted John for his testimony. At the very beginning, the Judeans sent priests and Levites from Jerusalem to learn John's identity. And when he told them, they asked why he was baptizing since he did not have the proper credentials (1:19, 25).

John was acknowledged as one who witnessed to the "truth," something very unusual in the Mediterranean world (5:33). Culturally speaking, precious few people outside one's close family have a right to the truth.

In John's Gospel, the Baptizer's function is exclusively that of a forensic witness. He came to bear witness to the light (1:7-8). He testified about the "one coming after me" (1:15). He is a consistent witness to Jesus' sinlessness. He points to Jesus as the stainless Lamb of God who takes away the sin of the world (1:29, 36). He boldly affirms Jesus' basic holiness when he says that he saw the Spirit of God on Jesus (1:32-33).

According to this Gospel, Jesus was baptized so that he might be revealed to Israel (1:31). Here it is John the witness rather than a "voice from heaven" that boldly proclaims that Jesus is none other than "Son of God" (1:34). The Mediterranean notion of a "witness" like John baffles Americans who relish "eyewitness" testimony and factual veracity. Mediterraneans, in turn, consider our investigative behavior and "the public's right to know" very rude and intrusive. At issue in both cultures is faith. What exactly does it mean?

Third Sunday in Ordinary Time
Matthew 4:12-23

The gospel for this Sunday proposes three topics for our consideration: the Baptizer, Jesus' ministry, and Jesus' disciples.

JOHN THE BAPTIZER

John is in prison; he will shortly be put to death. Matthew, Mark, and Luke make it clear that Jesus does not begin his own ministry until the Baptizer has completed his. In John's Gospel, Jesus begins his ministry before the Baptizer's imprisonment. All the Gospels indicate that the Baptizer had a successful and effective ministry in his own right. During Jesus' ministry, people often confused Jesus with or identified him as the Baptizer (Matt 1:13-14).

One plausible explanation for this confusion, proposed by contemporary scholars, is this. Moved to conversion by John's preaching, Jesus became his disciple. When John was imprisoned, Jesus ventured out on his own and gathered disciples (Matt 4:18-22) but continued to baptize and broaden his ministry (Matt 11:2-6). Soon he began to experience the ability to cast out demons and realized he had a distinctive ministry of his own (Matt 12:22-28). With this, Jesus stopped baptizing and came into his own.

JESUS' MINISTRY

After John's imprisonment, Jesus moves from Nazareth, his tiny hometown, to Capernaum, a larger crossroads town by the Sea of Galilee. He continues preaching John's message: "Repent, for the reign of heaven has approached" (Matt 4:17). Matthew encapsulates Jesus' ministry in a summary statement (v. 23): Jesus was teaching in the synagogues, preaching the good news, and healing.

A recent study by Heather McKay has shown that in Jesus' day the synagogue was a gathering place, like a modern community center, where males could meet on every day of the week to study or pray. Here Jesus read and listened to Torah, disputed and argued with others, but did not attend Sabbath services, for there were none at that time. For the ordinary first-century Jewish believer the Sabbath was not a day of worship; it was simply a day of rest. Modern-day scholars believe that the Christian practice of gathering to celebrate the Lord's Supper on the seventh day stimulated the development of Sabbath as a Jewish day of worship rather than the reverse, as is often thought.

As for his healing program, Jesus is clearly a "folk" healer and not a "professional." In contrast to the latter, Jesus attempts to heal people. He doesn't just talk about healing (see Third Sunday of Advent).

THE FIRST DISCIPLES

It would be wrong to think of Peter and his friends as "poor" and simple fisherfolk. In the first century, fishing on the Sea of Galilee developed into a major industry.

Large, extended families formed partnerships to engage in this business. Today's reading describes the partnership of Jonah and his sons, Simon and Andrew, as well as the partnership of Zebedee and his sons, John and James. Both families might have belonged to a larger partnership or conglomerate.

The boat discovered in Israel in 1986 when the Sea of Galilee was at an unusually low level is representative of the vessels owned by such as Jonah and Zebedee. Though it has been dubbed "Peter's boat," there is no way to confirm this.

Jesus' act of calling disciples is a common event in the Middle East. Usually, a person with a grievance invites people to join him in resolving the grievance. We don't know Jesus' grievance, but the disciples certainly did. This in part explains why they dropped everything to follow him. In unified groups there is strength. Moreover, this is the dry season. Farmers simply wait for the harvest. Fishing partners can leave the fishing to others for the time being. Now is the time to be out and about, to be seen and heard, to pursue group interests.

Such group orientation or connectedness permeates this reading as it does the entire Bible. The lives of the Baptizer, the disciples, and healed clients are entirely intertwined with Jesus.

Jesus' group-oriented culture lived by second nature what people like Samuel Gompers and Saul Alinsky would later have to teach to modern American individualists: Organize! Build your network! It's the only way you can win.

Fourth Sunday in Ordinary Time
Matthew 5:1-12

The most basic piece of information that a modern Western believer should learn about the Mediterranean world of Jesus is that honor, its central value, drives all behavior. Honor is a public claim to worth and a public acknowledgment by others of that claim.

BEATITUDES

The more than eighty "beatitudes" sprinkled throughout the Old and New Testaments are poetic sayings that present, encourage, and praise honorable behavior. Rather than "happy," "fortunate," or "blessed," the first word in each beatitude should more correctly be translated "truly honorable" or "highly esteemed" (is the one who behaves or thinks thus and so).

Moses concludes his praise of the tribes of Israel with this beatitude: "Truly honorable are you, O Israel! Who is like you, a people saved by the Lord, the shield of your help, and the sword of your triumph! Your enemies shall come fawning to you, and you shall tread on their backs" (Deut 33:29). Salvation by the Lord and public service from conquered enemies are publicly demonstrated and confirmed claims to honor.

A BEATITUDE CONTEST

As a person deeply embedded in his culture, Jesus, too, proposed honorable behavior in the familiar format of beatitudes. On one occasion reported by Luke, a woman, moved by his healing and teaching abilities, cried out: "Truly honorable or worthy of great esteem is your mother [the womb that bore you and breasts that nursed you]!". Jesus countered by saying: "Mothers [females] indeed should be esteemed, but even more honorable and worthy of esteem is the person [male or female] who hears the word of God and obeys it!" (Luke 11:27-28).

BEATITUDES IN JESUS' SERMON

Matthew (5–7) has gathered scattered pieces of Jesus' teaching and crafted them into an artificial sermon delivered on a hillside. Luke (6:17-49) reports an abbreviated version in a similar sermon delivered by Jesus on a plain. Both introduce the sermon with beatitudes.

Luke presents what were very likely the "original" three beatitudes Jesus spoke on that occasion; Matthew creatively expands them to eight. Matthew uses the appropriate grammatical form: third person singular ("honorable the one who . . ."). Luke gives them a more personally direct orientation by using the second person singular ("honorable are you who . . ."). Matthew's sermon will occupy our attention from now to the ninth Sunday in this cycle.

The three basic honorable and esteemed behaviors offered by Jesus are being poor, mourning, and hungering. "Poor" in the Bible is never an economic designation. It rather describes someone who has temporarily lost honorable status and must seek at all costs to regain but never surpass that status.

"Poor" thus refers to a revolving class of people. The customary association of poor with widows and orphans confirms this notion of losing status. Widows and orphans did not have to retain this position forever. Widows could remarry (see the serious discussion of "real" widows in 1 Tim 5:3-16); orphans could be reabsorbed into an extended family. Those who lost status were culturally obliged to regain it.

There are, however, two distinctive elements in Jesus' beatitudes. First, he says being poor constitutes true honor! Second, the passive voice in each beatitude ("will be comforted," "be filled," etc.) is a strategy used by our ancestors in the faith to avoid saying the name of God. Those who engage in social protest (mourning and fasting) will be comforted by whom? By God, of course! This grammatical usage in the Hebrew and Greek Bible is called, appropriately, the "theological or divine passive voice."

In Jesus' view, true honor and esteem are determined and bestowed by God, very publicly, for all to see. And the things that God considers truly honorable and worthy of praise are almost always the opposite of what human beings of any culture think.

Though modern American believers are not driven by the values of honor and shame as is the Mediterranean world, crises often indirectly reveal our genuine assessment of values. The survivors of a hurricane will say again and again that life is more precious than possessions. Yet given new opportunities, many would return to collecting material possessions and resuming conspicuous consumption. These are, after all, signs of American "honor."

Fifth Sunday in Ordinary Time
Matthew 5:13-16

SALT AND FIRE

Modern visitors to Israel who travel the road north from Jerusalem toward Shechem notice clay-ovens next to some houses along the roadside. Many prefer to cook in these outdoor ovens rather than on their electric or propane gas stoves. Ovens like these have been around since ancient times. In the biblical period each village had a common oven. Since villagers were often members of a very large, extended family, these common ovens were family ovens.

The common fuel for the oven was something that was more plentiful than wood: camel or donkey dung. One of the duties each young girl had to learn was to collect the dung, mix salt in it, and mould it into patties to be left in the sun to dry. In the Middle East and many Third World countries, such dung patties are still used as fuel today.

A slab of salt was placed at the base of the oven and upon it the salted dung patty. Salt has catalytic properties which cause the dung to burn. Eventually the salt slab loses its catalytic ability and becomes useless. Or as Jesus says, "It is good for nothing but to be thrown outside where it can still provide a sure footing in a muddy road."

This is the Mediterranean cultural imagery Jesus has in mind when he says: "You, my disciples, are the salt, that is, catalyst for the earth-oven." (In the Aramaic and Hebrew languages which Jesus spoke, one and the same word means "earth" and "clay-oven.")

AGONISTIC CULTURE

To be salt for the earth-oven is to start fires and make things burn. If Jesus' disciples do this, they will also be "light of the earth." The two images so masterfully joined show Jesus to be a clever and imaginative teacher.

This fire and light imagery reveals another basic Mediterranean cultural value. These people enjoy and engage in arguments on a regular, daily basis. Experts describe them as combative or agonistic.

How so? Honor, the public claim to worth, is almost always an invitation to an argument. The honor claim must be tested and verified before it can be affirmed. The public is more inclined to doubt or challenge the claim than grant it. This is how the people of this culture are "salty" folk, prone to starting the fires of intense argumentation.

Jesus is a master at it. He shows himself to be salty or catalytic by frequently resorting to his well-honed ability to insult people. For example, the word "hypocrite" occurs in Matthew thirteen times. Only Jesus uses the word, and he uses it mainly to insult his opponents, the Pharisees (6:2, 5, 16; 7:3-5; 15:7; 22:18; 23:13, 15, 24, 25, 27, 29-32; and 24:51).

The Greek word *hypokrites* means "actor." Jesus' frequent use of this word reveals two things. He seems to know a lot about the theater; and he views the Pharisees as nothing more than actors.

In recent years, archaeologists have uncovered a magnificent theater built by Herod Antipas in Sepphoris, that "big" city just an hour's walk away from Nazareth. Scholars conjecture that Joseph and Jesus might well have packed their lunch daily and walked to Sepphoris to ply their trade as artisans. Even if they didn't work on the theater, they could have learned a lot about it.

By calling the Pharisees "actors," Jesus charges that Scripture may provide the lines they quote, but it is hardly the script by which they live. "Do whatever they teach you and follow it, but do not do as they do, for they do not practice what they teach" (Matt 23:3). Jesus' other insults against the Pharisees include "blind guides" (23:16) and "blind fools" (23:17; compare with 5:21-26).

The salty Jesus started fires and created light. Some saw and understood. Others got burnt and put him to death. How can American believers imitate the salty Jesus? How would this work in American culture?

Sixth Sunday in Ordinary Time
Matthew 5:17-37

Matthew summarized Jesus' activities on his first tour of Galilee as teaching, healing, and preaching (4:23). He expands on Jesus' teaching in chapters 5–7, on his healing in 8–9, and on his preaching in 10 and the following chapters.

After redefining truly honorable behavior in the beatitudes, Matthew's Jesus announces his sermon's theme: the righteousness of his followers (or disciples, 6:19–7:27) must surpass that of the scribes (5:21-28) and the Pharisees (6:1-18).

Righteousness means proper and honorable relationships with other people, understood in this sermon to be other followers of Jesus and God. Matthew calls these people "brothers."

THE SCRIBES

The scribes, "Scripture scholars" of their day, specialized in the Law (Torah) and its proper observance. The Law was commonly summed up in commandments (Matt 22:34-40).

Historically, the purpose of the "ten" commandments was to regulate behavior between and among the Israelites. The idea was to minimize the potential annihilation of Israel as a result of internal, honor-driven blood feuds. In an honor-based society, murder, theft (which includes adultery), lying, and the like require retaliation. Jesus was killed in part because he so frequently shamed his antagonists (e.g., the scribes and Pharisees) in public arguments.

THE SERMON–PART ONE

In today's verses, Jesus takes aim at the scribes by reinterpreting the commandments. He offers his followers an honorable way out of situations that could lead to feuds and death. If it follows his interpretation, Jesus' faction will survive and attain its goals. *Murder* (vv. 21-26). Jesus forbids anger and insults that could escalate to murder. He forbids calling another "fool," though he hurls the word at the scribes and Pharisees in Matthew 23:17. For Jesus, squelching the feud even takes precedence over Temple worship! *Adultery and divorce* (vv. 27-32). The rigid and strictly enforced separation of men and women in this society made adultery almost impossible to conceal when it happened. Actually, adultery was less a result of passion than a deliberate attempt by one man to shame another.

Deuteronomy 22:22-24 called for the death of both parties, but the man often escaped while the woman's father and brothers would kill her for shaming *their* family. If the aggrieved husband took no action against his wife, he was considered a cuckold. If he took no action against the man, his own manhood was further questioned. Jesus says forget adultery as a means of challenging other men. The consequences are too devastating.

Divorce is equally disruptive to a tight-knit community like that of Jesus' followers. Since the ideal marriage partners were first cousins (Peter's mother-in-law was also his aunt), divorce could tear apart the villages in which these families lived and tried to make a living. Jesus says: "Forget divorce. Learn to live with your difficulty for the sake of family unity."

Matthew's community, however, seemed to allow divorce for reasons of "sexual irregularity" (see v. 32). The Greek words here and their Hebrew counterparts were matters of intense debate in the first century. Matthew's Jesus sides with the conservative school of Shamai which recognized sexual misconduct on the woman's part as the only reason for divorce, against the more progressive school of Hillel which allowed other reasons (e.g., if the wife spoils a meal).

Lying (vv. 33-37). The context here is selling. There was no food and drug commission to insure honesty. A seller would indirectly call God to witness his claim for his wares. Never mentioning God by name, the seller would swear "by my head, by my beard, on my life, by Jerusalem, etc." When he refused to make God explicit, conflict erupted. Jesus advised his followers to be honest and direct with one another at the market: yes or no.

Modern believers should keep two things in mind about these reflections. First, Jesus directs his interpretations solely to members of his in-group; his honor and shame society would disintegrate if everyone lived like this. Second, Jesus did not reject his society's honor-based system. He rather reshaped it to a more humane form.

American society is rooted in economics rather than honor and shame. How might human relationships in this system be reshaped to a more humane form?

Seventh Sunday in Ordinary Time
Matthew 5:38-48

REGAINING HONOR

Concluding his reinterpretation of the commandments, Jesus paints three scenes in which one disciple humiliated by another is urged to forego retaliation (vv. 38-41).

Being struck on the right cheek entails either a backhand slap from a right-handed person or an open-handed slap from a left-handed person. The left hand in the Middle East is reserved for toilet functions. It is a serious insult to place that hand on the table, use it in eating, or extend it to others. Both slaps are insulting (v. 39).

Having to resort to courts in the Middle East is very shameful. Arguments should be settled long before this stage. Jesus' recommendation to yield more (the tunic) than the plaintiff asks (the cloak) is astounding (v. 40). The cloak was absolutely essential not only as a piece of clothing but as a sleeping bag. To give this up too would leave one naked, a shameful condition to say the least.

Lastly, it was legal and customary for soldiers to force citizens to carry their military gear for one mile. In first-century, occupied Palestine, this soldier frequently was a fellow Israelite who turned mercenary. Carrying the gear was humiliation enough; being forced to do so by a traitorous fellow citizen was even more humiliating (v. 41).

In each instance, Jesus urges the humiliated disciple to suffer the shame and surrender the right to defend honor. Is the advice radical or culturally practical?

Middle Easterners are agonistic, combative. When threatened with dishonor, they will attempt to respond. Since all these insults happen in a very public arena, the attempt is normally sufficient. Usually others, certainly kin, will intervene to halt the insult process. This permits the shamed or dishonored one to be reconciled with the aggressor later when tempers cool.

Jesus' advice, therefore, is practical rather than radical. He urges relying upon others to defend against dishonor rather than seeking justice or shedding blood. It is preferable to preserve community rather than destroy it.

LOVING AND HATING

The feuding tendency in the Middle East guarantees that families will have many enemies. Such would be people who try to destroy honor, take land, undermine the family, or threaten the women. The ten commandments specifically prohibit these activities, but there is no commandment in the Bible to "hate one's enemies."

The Old Testament love commandment understands "neighbor" to be one's kin (Lev 19:17-18). An Israelite was not required to love non-kin.

But what precisely do love and hate mean in the Mediterranean world? Since these people were not at all introspective, psychology is of no help. Their attention was focused primarily and exclusively on external actions.

The most obvious external reality, to the Middle Easterner, is that human beings are group oriented. One belongs to a family, a village, a neighborhood, or a faction. Group membership bestows honor upon an individual and provides a sense of identity and a conscience. Apart from one's group, a person is nothing.

This combination of group orientation and inability to look inside causes people in this culture to be very concrete in their ways of thinking. Love and hate may be internal human emotions, but Mediterraneans focus exclusively on their external expression.

Love is therefore best translated as "attachment to the group" and hate as "detachment from or indifference to the group." Whether affection is present or not does not matter. To love God with all one's heart (Matt 22:37) means to be totally attached to him and demonstrate it in action. To love one's neighbor as one's self means to be as attached to the neighbor as to one's own family.

Luke's Jesus requires that his disciples "hate their family," that is, detach from them to join him and form a new family-like association (Luke 14:26).

Here Matthew's Jesus urges a more inclusive behavior among members of the in-group. Some new followers of Jesus may have been enemies of older followers (think of Paul's comment in Gal 1:23). In Jesus' group, there is no room for selective attachment and aloofness.

Christians of that time and ours have to be perfect in the same way that God is perfect (Matt 5:48). This means accepting everyone without discrimination, changing enemies into friends and even fictive kin. That's a mighty tall order in any culture.

Eighth Sunday in Ordinary Time
Matthew 6:24-34

THE SERMON–PART THREE

Cycle A passes over part two of Jesus' Sermon on the Mount (6:1-19) in which he reviews the elements of righteousness proposed by the Pharisees (almsgiving, prayer, and fasting) and demonstrates how his disciples should perform these same deeds with far less fanfare.

In part three (6:10–7:29), Jesus proposes assorted elements of righteousness that should distinguish his followers from the scribes (5:21-48) and Pharisees (6:19). The apparent jumble of topics in this section is actually orchestrated well around the first-century Mediterranean understanding of a human being as composed of three integrated, symbolic zones: heart-eyes (loving/hating two masters), mouth-ears (food and drink), and hands-feet (making clothes). When all three zones operate in coordination, the human person is righteous or well. When any of the zones malfunctions, the human person is not righteous or well.

SERVING TWO MASTERS

The typical situation in which a servant had two masters was when a father bequeathed one slave to two sons in the inheritance. The slave's problem is how to divide service equally or equitably between the two.

"Love" and "hate" must be understood in their Mediterranean sense: not as emotions but as degrees of attachment.

Our ancestors in the faith were not introspective and did not possess as sophisticated an awareness of internal states or emotions as modern Western believers do. They based themselves on external appearances and external considerations like attachment. Love means attachment, and hate means disattachment or alienation.

In addition, Middle Eastern society is strongly group oriented, so love (understood as attachment) links a person to a group. Jesus speaks of two masters, and we have explained that this means two sons. The culture would remind us that we are dealing with the entire families of two sons, that is, two groups. It is difficult to serve two groups in the Middle East. The modern Arab proverb says: "I against my brother; I and my brother against my cousins; but I, my brother, and my cousins against the world." One need only recall Cain and Abel, or Jacob and Esau, among other brothers in the Bible to realize the difficulty a slave would experience trying to serve two masters, that is, two groups or families. This is the context for interpreting Jesus' application: "You cannot serve God and wealth" (v. 24).

To achieve authentic righteousness, the disciple of Jesus must have a well-ordered and properly directed heart, one that is not divided.

PRESENT ANXIETY

Because they lived hand to mouth all the time, peasants could not afford the luxury of thinking ahead. They were totally absorbed in the challenge of living from moment to moment.

Jesus is not insensitive to the needs of peasants. Like all human beings, they were anxious about the basics of life: food, drink, and clothes (see Sir 29:21). Given the subsistence economy in which they lived, the unpredictability of nature, and the voracious taxes they were forced to pay, how could they think of anything but survival?

Jesus' advice is simple yet cleverly delivered. Without pointing his finger or naming names, he selects a masculine Aramaic noun (birds) and a feminine Aramaic noun (anemones, or lilies of the field) and urges men and women not to worry.

With the birds, Jesus associates men's work (sowing, reaping, harvesting); with the lilies of the field, women's work (spinning yarn, making clothes). Even success in these efforts cannot extend life beyond the measure set by God. Hence, one must trust in God the heavenly patron who knows the clients' basic needs and will meet them.

To achieve authentic righteousness, such as would surpass that sought by the scribes and Pharisees, Jesus urges his disciples to be certain that their mouth-ear and hands-feet zones are well aligned with their heart-eyes zone. All zones should be focused on God.

Modern Western believers will have to expend some effort to appreciate how our ancestors in the faith perceived human beings and human activity. Once the three-part symbolic understanding of the human body is grasped, it can easily be identified throughout the Bible from beginning to end. Our ancestors were deeply concerned with serving God single-mindedly. How would we describe American believers who focus single-mindedly on God?

Ninth Sunday in Ordinary Time
Matthew 7:21-27

People who speak in public know how important it is to prepare a good beginning and a good ending. Matthew's Jesus began his sermon with beatitudes, carefully crafted poetic statements proposing honorable behaviors for his followers. In antiquity, this would be a real "grabber." People would perk up their ears and listen. This speaker is good!

The conclusion is a sobering warning to listeners to consider how they will respond to the sermon. Perhaps they tuned Jesus out midway through his development. Some may have found it too pedestrian, others too progressive. Jesus tells the fates that will befall those who act upon his words and those who are unmoved by them.

PATRONAGE

In Middle Eastern culture, to call someone "Lord" is to recognize this individual as a personal patron. A patron chooses to treat clients (who are freely chosen) "as if" they were family members, that is, with favoritism. Everyone wants to be a client and even has specific patrons in mind, but the initiative comes always from the patron and never from the client. Fortunate clients who are selected by a powerful patron freely accept the obligation of doing what the patron expects and singing the patron's praises far and wide for all benefits they have received.

Matthew's Jesus warns those who have listened to his sermon that it is not enough to acknowledge him as patron, or broker with God, the ultimate patron. As the culture dictates, a client must fulfill the patron's wishes and behave in a way that pleases and honors the patron. Jesus the broker has specified what God the patron expects of clients. Now he urges that they behave appropriately and warns of fatal consequences if they do not.

BEING AND DOING

To appreciate the reason why Matthew's Jesus chose to conclude his sermon with this urgent call to action, one needs to understand how Mediterranean culture regards behavior. Generally speaking, this culture prefers the ideal to the real, words to action. The ideal is to speak respectfully to one's parent, even if such speech is a lie. "Yes, Father, I go to work in your vineyard," but truly I have no intention of going.

The ideal is to spew forth angry words but never take punitive action. "Woe to you Chorazin, Bethsaida! And you Capernaum will be brought down to hell" (cf. Matt 11:20-24), yet Jesus proceeds to pray calmly to the Father.

Experts identify this cultural reluctance to take effective action with "being." This word describes spontaneity rather than foresight, utter abandon rather than decisive, goal-directed action. People characterized by "being" spontaneously respond to the cues of the moment: to say the right thing, to dance when the music plays and stop when the music ceases, etc.

Americans generally behave very differently. They set goals and objectives and pursue them unwaveringly. Even on vacation, Americans tend to follow a plan, a set itinerary, a prearranged and guided tour. They are firmly committed to "doing," that is, achieving, and experience great difficulty just "being," just hanging out, letting the vacation unfold as it will. (Youngsters, of course, always resist the cultural expectations.)

JESUS AND HIS CULTURE

Throughout his ministry, Jesus appears to challenge his culture's preference for avoiding decisive action. He urges "doing" over "being." Here Jesus says it is not enough to honor God the patron with titles; one must do God's will. The Baptist challenged the Pharisees and Sadducees to "bear fruit" (Matt 3:8-10); Jesus does the same (13:23). Repeatedly Jesus plays variations on the theme of "Whoever does the will of my Father in heaven is my brother and sister and mother" (12:50; see also 21:28-32; 23:2; 24:45-51; 25:14-30, 31-46).

How surprising then to hear Jesus pray in the garden: "Father, thy will, not mine, be done" (26:39, 42, 44), and hear him chide the one who cut off the ear of the high priest's slave in a futile attempt to save Jesus (26:52-53). Jesus' decisive action is to do nothing! Jesus' understanding of "doing the will of God" should stimulate heated discussion among achievement-driven American believers who routinely log their accomplishments ("doing") on ever-growing résumés.

Tenth Sunday in Ordinary Time
Matthew 9:9-13

The account of the call of Matthew is situated in a cluster of ten healing stories which the evangelist has gathered in chapters 8 and 9. Though it is not one of these ten stories, healing is one of its motifs.

TOLLS

The scene is Capernaum, Jesus' own town (9:1). Capernaum was located on the northwest corner of the Sea of Galilee along the major road of international trade between Damascus and Egypt. Domestic trade among the towns and villages on the shores of the Sea of Galilee also had to pass through Capernaum.

Capernaum was well situated for collecting tolls which were levied on all goods in transit whether entering, leaving, or simply being transported across a district. Tolls also had to be paid for goods crossing over bridges or gates, or landings. Matthew was a toll collector who worked in the Capernaum custom house.

In Jesus' time, a toll collector was a native who contracted with Rome to collect the allotted tolls but paid them personally to Rome in advance and hoped to collect enough to make a profit. Historical evidence indicates that the gamble rarely paid off. The rich and the educated, a minuscule minority in Jesus' day, routinely criticized toll collectors. The poor rarely had anything on which duties could be levied and would likely sympathize with rather than criticize those who, like themselves, were trying to eke out a subsistence.

Jesus the village artisan (did he pay tolls?) invited Matthew the toll collector to his home, which very likely was located in Peter's father's complex at Capernaum. It is significant that Jesus' disciples and "many" other toll collectors and sinners came to eat dinner there. This indicates that Jesus had the ability to marshall sufficient resources to feed a large group. In a culture where ninety-five percent of the population existed at subsistence level, the ability to host such a meal suggests that Jesus was well connected with a network capable of providing provisions.

SICKNESS AND HEALING

Village life being as wide open as it was in antiquity (and still is today), the Pharisees clearly see what Jesus is doing. They hurl a public challenge against his honor by asking the quite likely embarrassed disciples: "Why does your teacher eat with tax collectors and sinners?"

Jesus, ever the master of riposte in these challenges, responds by citing a proverb. It is difficult for most Americans to appreciate such skill with proverbs, though other cultures like the Polish and segments of American culture like Appalachian and other southern storytellers are particularly adept at spontaneous, creative, and colorful responses. The proverb is: "Those who are well have no need of a physician, but those who are sick."

Before the very recent discovery, through the microscope, of germs and viruses, sickness was generally viewed as a loss of meaning in human life. Healing occurred when meaning was restored, even if the condition was not removed. In addition, the ancients never expected long-term effects. The condition could return a week or a month later.

Jesus draws an analogy between his association with toll collectors and sinners and the association of healers with sick people. Knowledge of the history of medicine helps a modern reader appreciate the analogy. In antiquity, healers preferred not to treat sick people because if the sick person died the healer might be put to death as well.

Jesus' activity contrasts with this cultural view because he touched the untouchables and associated with the outcasts in a way that good healers should have done but didn't. Moreover, sickness in ancient Israel nearly always entailed separation from the community until health returned. This was part of the understanding of purity and wholeness. In a group-oriented culture, separation from the community is a fate worse than death. Jesus' healing ministry in general always includes a restoration of the person to community, whether someone with repulsive scaly skin conditions (called "leprosy") or toll collectors who in general were a remarkably fair and honest group of people routinely stereotyped, condemned, and shunned by their peers.

Whom do contemporary American believers stereotype, condemn, and shun? How would Jesus respond?

First Sunday of Lent
Matthew 4:1-11

SPIRITS

The Mediterranean world lives by a deeply rooted belief in spirits who exist in numbers too huge to count and whose major pastime is interfering capriciously in daily human life. Contemporary Mediterranean cultures, like the Italian or Spanish, rely upon a broad range of amulets, formulas, or other symbols to ward off attacks from spirits.

Blue is a favorite color believed to be an especially powerful protection against spirits. People paint their window frames and door jambs blue or wear blue ribbons or clothes precisely for this reason. Others prefer red or scarlet, or wear specific medals, charms, or amulets that are guaranteed to impede attacks.

When the voice from heaven identified Jesus at his baptism as "my Son, the Beloved, with whom I am well pleased" (Matt 3:17), all the spirits heard this compliment. Every Mediterranean native knows what must and will happen next. Spirits will test Jesus to determine whether the compliment is indeed true, and just in case it might be true they will try to make him do something displeasing to God.

It is no surprise, then, that the very next scene Matthew presents is "the temptation." Jesus was full of the Holy Spirit. He was led by a good spirit into the wilderness, the normal habitat of spirits, where he did battle with an evil spirit, the devil.

What is surprising in Matthew's narrative is that Jesus is not reported to be wearing blue garments or using an amulet or even special formulas for protection. Rather, he engages in direct, one-on-one dialogue with this evil spirit in a Scripture-quoting contest.

THE TEMPTATION

Three times Jesus is tempted to do something that would make him a displeasing son. Three times Jesus replies with a quotation from Scripture (Deut 8:3; 6:16; 6:13) to vanquish the temptation. The devil also quotes Scripture to Jesus (Ps 91:11-12) but still does not succeed in tripping him up. Jesus wins the contest, and the devil leaves him.

The temptation story is based upon and carefully crafted after the pattern of Israel's temptations in the desert during its Exodus from Egypt. Matthew arranged the temptations differently from Luke in order to end with the high mountain as the scene of the final temptation (see Cycle C, First Sunday of Lent). Mountains are important symbols in Matthew. They identify places of revelation, places where the Father of the Son gives teaching to human beings.

Clearly, the story of Jesus' victory over the devil is not intended by Matthew as a model for baptized Christians who also have to battle against evil spirits. No Christian possesses the powers that Jesus is here tempted to misuse.

Matthew's purpose in this story is to present Jesus as the faithful and obedient Son of God, just as he was presented in the baptism story (Matt 3:13-17). The implied contrast of the obedient son, Jesus, with the disobedient son, Israel in the Exodus story, is deliberate.

Those among Matthew's first readers who asked: "Why should I believe in Jesus?" are given culturally appropriate answers. Jesus is a model of obedience to God. He emerges victorious from his combat with the devil. He can safeguard and maintain his honor and avoid shame. Until his arrest, trial, and death, no one—human or spirit—succeeds in shaming him, tripping him up, or causing him to fall from his stated position and goals. This is the consequence of unflinching obedience to God.

Americans in general do not believe that spirits cause them any problems. This cultural conviction is what made the comedian Flip Wilson's character, Geraldine, so amusing every time she resorted to her favorite excuse: "The devil made me do it!"

But Americans do understand power. They especially understand and resent abuse of power by those who should wield it for the benefit of others. Scholars point out that in the Gospels Jesus wields no power at all except in regard to spirits and demons. The story of Jesus' refusal to abuse the power he possessed offers Americans something very relevant to ponder.

Second Sunday of Lent
Matthew 17:1-9

Throughout his Gospel, Matthew is intent upon presenting Jesus as a Moses-like figure. Here Jesus' face shines like Moses' did (Exod 34:29-30). Moses is named before Elijah.

Scholars agree that it is impossible to say exactly what "really" happened in this event in Jesus' ministry. Mediterranean culture, however, offers some helpful insights.

CULTURAL BACKGROUND

(1) Honor, the main Mediterranean cultural value. Jesus' demonstrated power over demons gave him a solid claim to honor in his culture. This ability stood in contrast to his known origins. Remember Nathanael's sarcastic question to Philip: "Can anything good come out of Nazareth?" (John 1:46).

(2) Power and shame. Jesus' power over demons also placed him in jeopardy. No one ever denied the reality of this power (Matt 13:54), but many leaders wondered about the source of Jesus' authority (Matt 21:23). Some concluded that he was in cahoots with the devil (Matt 9:34).

If Jesus does not possess legitimate power and authority, then he is arrogating to himself something to which he has no right. This is very shameful.

(3) Power and politics. To complicate matters, power belongs to the realm of politics. In the Gospels, Jesus' healings and exorcisms are viewed by all—friend and foe alike—as political activities. This is the concern behind the puzzlement in Matthew 21:23. Unapproved political activities could lead to death.

Jesus was not unaware of these potential consequences of his ministry. He told his disciples that "he must go to Jerusalem and suffer many things from the elders and chief priests and scribes, and be killed, and on the third day be raised" (Matt 16:21). Fully accepting the risk of his ministry, Jesus was also convinced that God would grant him ultimate, honorable vindication. He would be raised by God! What an honor!

THE TRANSFIGURATION

Only Matthew refers to this experience as a vision (17:9), but this is a most important piece of information. Modern psychological anthropology points out that alternative states of consciousness like visions and dreams are normal human experiences common to the majority of the world's cultures. Cultures in which these are not so common, like the contemporary United States, are the ones to be explained.

In Matthew's version of the transfiguration, Jesus is obviously experiencing an alternative state of consciousness. Peter, James, and John are participants in this experience, during which they gain a clearer understanding of Jesus as one who lived on the brink of shame all the time but still maintained a position of favor with the Father. In all cultures, altered states of consciousness are normal means of learning new information.

These three chosen disciples realized that contrary to occasional appearances and impressions, Jesus was an honorable person whose activities were pleasing to God. Jesus' firm conviction that God would restore his honor by raising him from the dead (see Matt 16:21; 17:23; 20:19) was not a simple whistling in the dark. It was rooted in God's steadfast loving kindness, experienced in alternative consciousness.

In Matthew's lifetime, many actual and potential Mediterranean believers in Jesus were troubled by his shameful death. If this man's life and ministry were pleasing to God, why did it seem that God abandoned him?

Matthew's portrayal of Jesus as another Moses shows that God no more abandoned Jesus than he abandoned Moses. Matthew exhorts his Church to stand under the Lordship of the risen Lord who is a second Moses and lawgiver to his

Church. Jesus will come at the end to judge that Church according to the new or better righteousness that he taught, just like Moses, on a mountain (see Matt 5–7, especially 5:1, 20).

What does the transfiguration story say to contemporary Western believers? In his honor and shame culture, Jesus maintained steadfast trust in God no matter how shameful his life experiences appeared. To a large degree, he had no other choice in his culture. But his faith and trust paid off: God restored honor to him in a way that no human ever could have.

In our very different culture, where self-reliance is highly valued, it is equally challenging to trust in God, especially when we feel we are fully in control of our life and destiny. Would that the behavior of all believers in every culture would merit divine approval: "This is my beloved, with whom I am well pleased. Listen to what this person says!"

Third Sunday of Lent
John 4:5-42

A popular proverb says: "Familiarity breeds contempt." In the case of Bible stories, familiarity blunts sensitivity and often blocks proper understanding. Anyone familiar with Mediterranean culture immediately identifies shocking and jarring elements in this story.

WHAT IS WRONG WITH THIS PICTURE?

Scholars doubt that this event ever took place in the life of Jesus. There is no Synoptic evidence for a ministry in Samaria. Indeed, Jesus forbade it (Matt 10:5). After the resurrection, John was involved in the mission to Samaria (Acts 8:1-8), and the Johannine community contained Samaritan believers. This scene was, therefore, likely read back into Jesus' lifetime from the history of the Johannine community.

From a Mediterranean cultural perspective, there are other irregularities that offer new insight into the story.

(1) Wrong place, wrong time. The Mediterranean world is divided according to gender. Women have their places (kitchen, home); men have theirs (outdoors, the fields, the gate, the marketplace). The well is space common to both men and women, but they ought not to be there at the same time. Women can use the place only in morning or evening. Here, the woman comes to the well at noon (v. 6). Wrong time, and therefore wrong place.

Likely she comes at this hour because the women of her village shun her for her shameless behavior (five husbands, now living with someone other than her husband, vv. 16-18).

She comes to the well at an hour when other women will be properly elsewhere. She is alone.

(2) Speaking to a strange man in public. Even the woman admits this irregularity. "How is it that you, a Judean man, ask me, a Samaritan woman, for a drink?" (v. 9). Culture indicates that the problem is not different ethnic heritage but different genders. For a man to speak to an unchaperoned woman in a public place is very suspicious. The disciples take note and are shocked! They did not dare to ask the obvious cultural questions: "What do you want from her?" or "Why are you talking to her?" (v. 27).

(3) Talking to other men in a public place. After her discussion with and enlightenment by Jesus, the woman went to the village marketplace, the place reserved for men; women should not enter there when men are present. And she admits to them that Jesus knew what they all knew: that she was a shameless woman, who behaved shamelessly regarding cultural rules governing proper behavior between men and women (notably marriage).

WHAT IS THE EVANGELIST INTENDING TO SAY WITH THIS SCENE?

Clearly, a cultural subversion is taking place. Modern social scientists would call this a cultural innovation. John seems to be confirming new roles for women in his community.

Jesus not only talks with the woman, but in a carefully orchestrated, seven-part dialogue (each speaks seven times) he guides her progressively from ignorance to enlightenment, from misunderstanding to clearer understanding. She is the most carefully and intensely catechized person in this entire Gospel!

Though the woman demonstrates her brazenness in discussing "masculine," political-religious topics ("Messiah" and "Temple") with Jesus, he accepts her questions and answers them rather than steering her back to "feminine" topics. Revolutionary indeed!

Some scholars go so far as to claim that this mixed-breed woman is the first disciple in John's Gospel. They suggest that Jesus himself commissioned her when he said: "Go call your husband, and come back" (v. 16).

Others disagree and note the following contrast. The evangelist reports: "Many Samaritans from that city believed in Jesus because of the woman's testimony" (v. 39). But the village men in the narrative offer a left-handed compliment: "It is no longer because of what you said that we believe, for we have heard for ourselves" (v. 42).

Comparing and contrasting women's place in ancient Mediterranean and contemporary Western culture is instructive in its own right but ought not deflect attention from the woman's astonishing and rapid insight into who Jesus really is: "Judean [a scornfully pronounced identification]," "sir," "prophet," and "Messiah," leading ultimately to the village's recognition of Jesus as "Savior of the world." Would that all believers could progress as insightfully and rapidly as she and her village.

Fourth Sunday of Lent
John 9:1-41

Secrecy, deception, and lying are integral parts of Mediterranean culture and valued strategies for maintaining and preserving honor. Westerners are often baffled by this.

Recall the shock one year after the end of the Gulf War when Americans learned that the young girl who testified to a congressional committee that Iraqi soldiers took Kuwaiti babies out of incubators and threw them on the floor to die had deceived the committee. She hid her al-Sabbah (the ruling family of Kuwait) identity from committee members and completely fabricated this report. It never happened.

Today's gospel reading about healed blindness reveals glimpses of secrecy, deception, and lying in Mediterranean culture.

BLINDNESS

While the ancient world certainly knew blindness as a real physical condition, they seemed to consider it no worse than ignorance or a stubborn refusal to understand. Luke writes of Jesus: "on *many* that were blind he bestowed sight" (7:21) but he reports only one specific healing of a physically blind person (18:35-43)! On the other hand, Luke-Acts reports many instances of people who refused to "see or understand" and people who chose to "see or understand." There thus seems to be greater interest in metaphorical than physical blindness.

In John's report of the man who was blind from birth, both motifs are played out strongly. It is futile to argue about the man's physical condition. He and his parents said he had been physically blind; others doubted or denied it. But the controversy stirred by the man's cure ranges beyond physical blindness to deception and lying. Here is a fruitful area for reflection.

SECRECY, DECEPTION, AND LIES

In the Mediterranean cultural world, everyone minds everyone else's business. Life is lived in the open, in the public eye, and privacy is practically nonexistent (see Luke 4:42). It would be impossible to live in such a world if one could not keep at least some part of one's personal life hidden from others. This is where secrecy, deception, and lying come into play. Families try to keep family matters hidden or secret within the inner sanctum of the home. Deception and lies are strategies regularly used to keep information from others (see John 7:1-10).

The culture permits and expects children to try to snoop out the truth (see Matt 19:13-15) by wandering in and out of the adult world. At the same time, adults instruct their children never to report the inner workings of their own family while snooping on others.

THE HEALED BLIND MAN

After the healing, there is confusion about the man's identity. "It is he," said some, while others countered: "No, but it is someone like him." And the healed man kept insisting: "I am the man!" (v. 9). In a world without photo IDs and social security numbers, proving personal identity is a real challenge.

The Pharisees also seem to accept the healing as a fact (v. 15) but are divided about Jesus' identity: is he a man "from God" or not (v. 16)?

Some hostile Judeans doubt that the healed man ever was blind at all (v. 18)! His parents confirm their son's congenital blindness but evade the hostile questions about the healing. "Ask him. He is old enough to speak for himself."

Hostility and enmity toward Jesus are certainly part of this story. At the same time, there are sincere people really struggling to "see" and "understand" what has happened or who Jesus really is. The prevalence of secrecy, deception, and lying in this culture explains skepticism as a natural part of day-to-day life, and even make hostility and enmity understandable if not excusable.

The concluding verses (39-41) illustrate how masterfully Jesus worked within his culture. When needed, he used his powers to heal. In the debates that followed, he drew on his culture's strengths and weaknesses.

The fluctuation between physical and metaphorical blindness is common in the gospel traditions. Jesus' point here, as always, is that physical blindness would be understandable and preferable to the willful metaphorical blindness of those who refuse to believe in him. The contemporary popular song captures the idea very well: "There are none so blind, as those who will not see."

Fifth Sunday of Lent
John 11:1-45

A recent flight across the Atlantic was enlivened by reading an article in the Journal of the Royal College of Physicians. A physician and his theologian wife argued that from a medical perspective, Jesus did not die and rise from the dead. He merely collapsed and was resuscitated. Though these authors did not extend their hypothesis further, others have said the same about Lazarus.

The often helpful insights of modern medical science forget that the story of the raising of Lazarus is a "sign" in John's Gospel and not the medical notes of a coroner. In John's Gospel, there are seven "signs" that are primarily intended to stir faith in Jesus (2:11). Sometimes they do the very opposite (11:47-48).

LIFE AT TWO LEVELS

According to the story, Lazarus has died. Martha and others believe that had he arrived on time, Jesus might have prevented Lazarus' death or raised him up immediately. As John writes this story for his community, Martha represents that grieving community in asking the perennial question: "If Jesus gave us eternal life, why are believers still dying?" John's story offers a challenging response.

THE TIME OF JESUS

Jesus' raising of Lazarus from the dead after four days in the tomb stirred the admiration of some. "Many of the Judeans who . . . had seen what Jesus did, believed in him" (11:45). But others (namely, the chief priests and Pharisees) "planned— from that day on—to put him to death" (11:53). This was the straw that finally broke the camel's back. Jesus' fate is sealed. As the story continued, Jesus was tried, crucified, buried, and raised, and in his resurrection all believers have eternal life. But this belief was often shaken by normal events.

JOHN'S COMMUNITY

Like other New Testament communities, that of John experienced a great crisis of faith when any believer died. If Jesus gave us eternal life, why must we still die? The evangelist therefore has added symbolic interpretations to this story of the death of Lazarus, the faithful disciple whom Jesus loved (11:5, 36).

Martha represents the community with its real but inadequate faith: "Lord, if you had been here my brother would not have died." If only Jesus had not left at his ascension, he would still be with the community and believers wouldn't die. After all, whatever Jesus asks of the Father will be given, won't it? (v. 22).

John's Jesus must correct this misunderstanding. He is indeed "the resurrection and the life" (v. 24). But resurrection does not mean the restoration of life to a corpse, it entails rather a transformation of life.

Moreover, the eternal life that Jesus gives his followers does not abolish death but rather transcends it. To continue to believe this firmly is the challenge posed to the survivors by each believer's death.

Through Martha, Jesus addresses believers of all times: "Do you believe this?" Her perfect answer ought to echo through the ages: "Yes, Lord, I believe that you are the Messiah, the Son of God, the one coming into the world."

Faith in the risen Jesus is not fully developed until it enables a believer to face physical death with the firm confidence that the present possession of eternal life is not simply a pledge of resurrection on the last day but is rather a present and continuing participation in the life of the ever-living Jesus now, at this moment. Those who believe in Jesus never truly die.

What scientifically minded Western believers must recognize in the story of Lazarus is that Martha pronounces her confession of faith as a response to Jesus who reveals himself as the resurrection and the life. Her faith does not depend upon or flow from seeing her brother raised from the dead. Proof begets knowledge; faith does not rest on proof.

The insights of our prescientific, Mediterranean ancestors in the faith are like Hamlet's humbling comment: "There are more things in heaven and earth, Horatio, than are dreamt of in your philosophy [or science]" (*Hamlet,* act 1, scene 6, line 167).

Passion Sunday
Matthew 26:14–27:66

THE DEVELOPMENT OF THE PASSION STORY

The passion story of Jesus is the oldest part of the Christian tradition to be preserved. Paul reports the earliest form of this tradition: Christ died for our sins, was buried, was raised on the third day, appeared to Cephas, and then to the Twelve (1 Cor 15:3b-5). This ancient tradition is remarkable for its brevity and lack of detail.

To it Paul added other appearances: to more than five hundred believers at one time, to James, to all the apostles, and lastly to Paul (1 Cor 15:6-8). The emphasis is entirely upon appearances of the risen Jesus; there are no details about Jesus' suffering and death.

As the first generation of Christians began to die, a short narrative of Jesus' passion developed: He was arrested, tried, and crucified. People yearned to know still more, so the narrative was elaborated to include the anointing, the Supper, and the plots to arrest him.

By the time the evangelists began to compose their works, two major developments of the longer story of Jesus' passion had evolved. One version, represented in Mark and Matthew, is characterized by fulfillment themes. Psalms 22 and 69, Isaiah, and other Scripture passages were fulfilled in Jesus' experience.

The other version, represented in Luke and John, featured many more words of Jesus. If one compares the accounts of the Supper, Mark and Matthew present a simple scene with

Jesus speaking just a few sentences, Luke adds more dialogue, and John omits the institution of the Eucharist entirely but reports four chapters of dialogue between Jesus and his apostles! Scholars claim that this kind of development is rooted in "pietism."

What prompted this gradual development of the passion story? Though it may seem backwards to us, the passion story was a normal follow-up to the resurrection. The fact that Jesus was raised by God was the only thing the early Mediterranean Christians needed to strengthen their faith in Jesus.

SUFFERING AND SHAME

He had died a shameful death, one reserved for the worst of criminals. Even though he died in the best Mediterranean manly tradition, this manner of death wiped out with one stroke all the good he had done. *If* Jesus truly were beloved of God, God would not have allowed him to be overcome by his enemies.

But God turned this Mediterranean, human way of thinking completely upside down. By raising Jesus from the dead, God honored Jesus more than anyone ever could have. He obliterated Jesus' shame.

From this vantage point, the evangelists were able to reinterpret the passion story. While it reports seemingly shameful events like betrayal, false witnesses, kangaroo courts, bullyism, and the like, a more careful reading shows that Jesus is master of his fate throughout the story. He knows he is in the right, he trusts that God will vindicate him. Jesus is like every other innocently suffering person in the history of Israel: absolutely confident that God will set it all aright.

Yet even if one misses this hindsight interpretation in the gospel stories, at the purely cultural level Jesus is presented as an extraordinary hero. Like the authentic Mediterranean male, he takes the best punch his enemies can throw without flinching, crying, or fainting. He endures flogging, verbal insult, crowning with thorns, crucifixion itself—but does not shriek.

In Matthew, the only sentence Jesus speaks ("My God, why have you forsaken me?") is a prayerful response to the taunts of all around who claim that God has abandoned him. These words are the opening of Psalm 22, a prayer filled with the agony of a believer.

The cultural convictions of modern Western readers frequently cause them to miss the point of this reading. In our culture, where suffering is a nuisance and pain can readily be avoided by cleverness or medicine, it is difficult to admire Mediterranean manliness demonstrated in endurance. In our culture, where science comes close to being a major "religion" for many, the significance of being raised by God from the dead, being restored to honor after devastating shame, is lost in the quest for logical meaning and apologetic proofs.

How can we imitate Jesus' obedience in a very different cultural world?

Easter Sunday
John 20:1-9

In this version of an "empty tomb" story that undergirds Christian belief in the resurrection of Jesus, it is difficult to miss the special importance John assigns to Mary Magdalene.

While Matthew, Mark, and Luke report that a group of women went to the tomb on Sunday morning, only John reports that Mary Magdalene came alone, unaccompanied by other women. From a cultural perspective, this is very unusual behavior. A woman alone outdoors is an anomaly. Theologians believe that this is John's way of highlighting the Magdalene's special importance. She is, in his mind, a "typical" figure who represents a special character trait or reflects a certain theological position.

MARY'S KNOWLEDGE

Mary's initial response to the empty tomb is to suspect theft (see Matt 28:13-15; 27:62-66). This is implied in her report to the disciples: "They have taken the Lord . . . we do not know where they have laid him (see John 20:2, 13, 15).

Twice Mary admits that she "does not know," a major theme in John's Gospel. In general, "not knowing" is not a problem in John's Gospel because Jesus can instruct these "ignorant" ones and bring them to light. This is clearly what he does with the Samaritan woman at the well (4:7-26) and with Thomas (14:5).

But it is a problem not to "be in the know." Jesus chides Nicodemus, a leader, for precisely this shortcoming: "Are you a teacher of Israel and yet you *do not know* these things [about being born from above, of the spirit]?" (3:10). Though she admits that she is not in the know, Mary is brought by Jesus to a very special knowledge. Jesus tells her "whither" he has gone: "I am ascending to my Father and your Father, to my God and your God" (20:17).

This special knowledge, given by Jesus uniquely to Mary Magdalene, makes her a "typical" or representative character. Just as Nathanael is a typical character who is not misled by those who object to the message about Jesus but comes and sees for himself, so Mary is typical in becoming now an insider, someone definitely "in the know."

She can even be called a beloved disciple because she receives a special revelation. Mary Magdalene stands out as an "enlightened" person in this Gospel. She does not depend upon the group or any other person for her special knowledge about Jesus, as Simon Peter depended upon his brother Andrew (1:35-40). In this, Mary is very different from the ordinary folk in this Gospel.

MARY'S EXPERIENCE

Mary Magdalene is typical from yet another perspective. In the Mediterranean world, status is ordinarily gained by ascription. This means that people gain their status by birth or inheritance. Human effort is of no avail in obtaining or improving status, but failed human effort can result in loss of status, or shame.

Genealogies are important not because they trace a family tree, but because they prove a Mediterranean person's claim to honor and status.

But Mary's special status in this Gospel does not derive from an appointment by the earthly Jesus but rather from her experience of the risen Jesus. In highlighting this aspect of Mary's experience, John is underscoring a motif that runs through his Gospel: whatever is earthly, material, of the flesh, is of no avail (6:63; 8:23). The "spiritual" is important, that which is out of the ordinary. Mary thus has spiritual status. As a typical figure, she becomes an extraordinary person.

Finally, in this Gospel the Samaritan woman at the well (4:49); Martha, a "beloved disciple" (11:5, 25); and now Mary Magdalene (20:17) all receive special revelations from Jesus. While the Samaritan woman and Martha went and called others to Jesus, they were not "officially commissioned" to do so in the same way that Jesus formally commanded Mary Magdalene: "Go to my brothers and say to them . . . ."

Despite their different kinds of commissions from Jesus, the three women enjoy rather high status in John's community. This is all the more significant in Mary Magdalene's case because her role is unusual and rather controversial.

How did our allegedly patriarchal ancestors ever accept the help of women in making sense out of an empty tomb? How did these Middle Eastern women succeed without quotas and affirmative action laws? Believers will find stimulating help in Jerome H. Neyrey's insightful booklet, *The Resurrection Stories* (see Recommended Readings).

Second Sunday of Easter
John 20:19-31

Of the two themes contained in this gospel story, that of the so-called doubting Thomas has been treated in *The Cultural World of Jesus Sunday by Sunday,* Cycle C (Second Sunday of Easter). Here we focus on the "vocation commissioning" of the apostles.

A common literary form appears throughout the Bible to describe the divine vocation of a great patriarch or prophet who is called to be the leader of God's people. It can be found in the vocation stories of Moses (Exod 3:4–4:9); Gideon (Judg 6:11-36ff.); Jeremiah (1:1-10); and Jesus' disciples (Matt 28:16-20; Luke 24:33-53; John 20:19-27; 21:1-19).

The complete form has five elements which can be identified in today's passage as follows.

INTRODUCTION

The setting for Jesus' appearance to commission the disciples is a house with locked doors in which the Eleven are gathered. In Jesus' nosey Mediterranean society, people suspect that those who gather behind locked doors are up to no good. Unlocked doors allow the children, the official "spies" or "snoops" in the village, to wander in and out of homes at will, keeping everyone on the up and up.

For this reason, John notes that the Eleven were hiding nothing but were rather protecting themselves against attacks from Judeans who did not believe in Jesus. This observation is truer of John's time (especially after 90 C.E.) than of

Jesus'. The locked doors have no relationship to Jesus' ability to penetrate them without opening them.

CONFRONTATION, REACTION, REASSURANCE

The sudden appearance of the risen Jesus (confrontation) startles the disciples (reaction), requiring that Jesus set them at ease: "Peace be with you!" (reassurance).

COMMISSION

Three points characterize this commissioning ceremony: (1) the commission is formal ("As the Father has sent me, so I send you," 20:21); (2) they are to preach repentance and forgive sins (20:22-23); and (3) the commission is confirmed by Jesus' sending of the Holy Spirit (20:22).

Generally speaking, sin according to John is failure to believe in Jesus as the one sent by the Father. This is the basic meaning behind the declaration heard in the liturgy at communion time: "Behold the Lamb of God, behold the one who takes away the sin [note the singular!] of the world!" The Johannine community had a tradition about forgiveness of sin in this sense (1 John 1:9; 2:19), a tradition for dealing with the sinfulness of its members.

The forgiveness of sin mentioned here in verses 22-23 is quite different. It implies the task of bringing new members into the community. From this perspective, the idea of this verse is similar to the instructions of Jesus in Matt 28:19 and Luke 24:47.

OBJECTION

It falls to Thomas rather than the newly commissioned apostles to raise an objection. He implies that the apostles may have suffered hallucination, an alternative state of consciousness. He expresses strong doubt about the reality of the risen Jesus. His demand to stick his fingers into the wounds of Jesus in the story created about him by John is well known.

REASSURANCE, SIGN

Ordinarily, deities would be miffed by such objections, but in the heavenly commissions reported in the Bible the divine response is very different. In this story, Jesus returns once again to the disciples chiefly to reassure Thomas, and through him all followers who experience difficulty believing without seeing. The sign is the invitation to Thomas to stick his fingers in the wounds as he wished (20:27). Jesus' gesture works; Thomas is convinced.

Modern Western believers have become rather familiar with "literary forms" in the Bible over the past twenty-five years. Parable stories, healing stories, the letters of Paul–all these and more are reported in the Bible in stock, stereotypical (i.e., unchanging) forms.

After learning about these many forms and their structure, believers (and often even preachers) say: "So what? What does this mean in the real world?"

Today's gospel describes how Jesus commissioned his followers to bring new members into God's covenant community. He had done this earlier in the farewell discourse (13:20; 17:18). Careful study of the literary form and its structure convinces scholars that the commission is addressed to all disciples and is not limited just to the Eleven. All believers are commissioned to bring new members into the community.

How does each one of us respond to this commission?

Third Sunday of Easter
Luke 24:13-35

This story, unique to Luke, tells of Jesus' appearance to two disciples who had given up their faith and departed from the group of Jesus' disciples. They were travelling from Jerusalem to Emmaus when the risen Jesus joined them, seemingly out of nowhere, opened their eyes to the Scriptures, and then revealed himself to them in the breaking of the bread.

Three themes emerge from a careful reading or hearing of this passage. First, Jesus is intent upon teaching these disheartened travellers the "correct" meaning of God's Scriptures. They knew the Scriptures but didn't understand them. Jesus himself preaches the very first Easter sermon.

Second, the meal has the overtones of a Eucharist and serves to complement Jesus' scriptural instruction on the road. The experience is uplifting and "heartening."

Third, Luke consistently tries to portray the followers of Jesus as unified in belief and at table. He illustrates this at the Last Supper (Luke 22:14-28, meal plus table-talk instruction) as well as among the new group of Jesus' followers after Peter's Pentecost speech (Acts 2:42; see also 20:11). Clearly Luke understands the Eucharist as a rite that symbolizes full communion of mind and heart.

Where exactly is Emmaus? This question helps move our reflection still further as we explore the "correct" understanding of Scripture.

Pilgrims to modern-day Israel are shocked to learn that as many as six sites are identified as "Emmaus." Here are the four more popular ones.

(1) Latrun. The tradition of identifying this place as Luke's Emmaus reaches back to the historian Eusebius (330). Christians may have lived here since early times, but the first known Christian is Julius Africanus who in 221 obtained for this village from Rome the rights of a Roman city and a new name, Nicopolis. The Byzantine tradition never doubted this identification, but it seems to have been forgotten when a plague wiped the village out in 639. Modern archaeologists doubt that this is the place mentioned in Luke. It certainly is 160 stadia (31 km) from Jerusalem (see Luke 24:13), but other ancient manuscripts of Luke read 60 stadia, suggesting Abu Ghosh or Qubeiba as the more likely spot.

(2) Abu Ghosh. This is the village on the Jaffa road where the ark of the covenant rested for twenty years (1 Sam 6:21–7:2), but in Old Testament times it was located atop the hill, not in the valley. The crusaders, our embarrassingly ignorant, Christian, warrior-ancestors in the faith, did not know about Latrun. So in typical crusader style, they measured 60 stadia from Jerusalem and identified the nearest village as Emmaus. When the crusaders were beaten in 1187 at the Battle of the Horns of Hattin, this place lost its importance mainly because travellers to Jerusalem used a different route. The identity of Emmaus was eventually transferred to Qubeiba.

(3) Qubeiba. Between 1114 and 1164, the Canons of the Holy Sepulchre founded a village here to intensify the agriculture of the region from which they drew sustenance. They named it Parva Mahomeria, perhaps because of a Muslim shrine already here (*el-Qubeiba* = "a little cupola"). As frequently happens in the Holy Land, later pilgrims assumed this place was related to the life of Christ, and since it was sixty stadia from Jerusalem, they identified it as Emmaus.

(4) "Most probable" Emmaus. After the Jewish War against Rome in 66-70 C.E., Vespasian assigned eight hundred discharged veterans to live in a place called "Emmaus," located about thirty stadia, or four miles, from Jerusalem. Their encampment completely overshadowed the little town, and the site was given the name (until recently) Qoloniya. Abandoned in 1948, it was located near contemporary Motza. The round trip between Jerusalem and this place is sixty stadia, or

about seven miles, half of this being a very plausible distance allowing the disciples to get up from table right after supping with Jesus and to return immediately to Jerusalem (Luke 24:33).

This brief archaeology and geography lesson suggests that those who read the Bible or understand their beliefs too literally will surely encounter serious problems. Jesus was able to "correct" the misunderstanding of his followers only because they were already familiar with the Scripture about him. Modern scholarship offers similar assistance to interested contemporary believers. "Blind" faith, after all, is a curious gift to return to the creator of human intelligence.

Fourth Sunday of Easter
John 10:1-10

In the Mediterranean world of Jesus, sheep are much more than cute, cuddly animals (the Bible never calls them stupid). They provide food, but more importantly, they are pervasive and powerful symbols. Sheep and goats are interpreted and treated as symbols of the internal differences peculiar to this world.

Since this world is strictly divided along gender lines, sheep and goats symbolize men and women respectively, and therefore also honor and shame.

In today's gospel, Jesus begins by describing a scenario concerning raising sheep in first-century Palestine. Then he applies the scenario to himself and his ministry. (See Thirty-Fourth Sunday in Ordinary Time for another reflection on sheep and goats.)

THE SCENARIO

Jesus begins by contrasting the honorable or noble shepherd with the "thief, bandit, and stranger" (vv. 1, 5, 8, 10). That the disciples did not understand is not surprising. An honorable shepherd in that culture is an oxymoron, a contradiction in terms. All shepherds were viewed as thieves, as men who exposed their women to shame by leaving them uncared for while they pastured the sheep, and as immoral men who found pleasure in sheep while absent from their wives.

Jesus, however, carefully spells out the characteristics of an honorable shepherd. (1) He enters by the door instead of sneaking in some other way. (2) The gatekeeper recognizes him as the genuine shepherd of this flock and permits him to enter. Others would be barred. Recalling the large, extended nature of the Middle Eastern family, even the gatekeeper role makes sense. Each family had its own flock, but pasturing their flocks together required a common pen where they might be kept. One kinsperson who knew all the shepherds was designated gatekeeper.

(3) He leads the sheep in and out. This characteristic is more difficult to appreciate. People who raise sheep insist that shepherds do not lead sheep. They rather walk behind and urge them forward thus being able to keep an eye out for wayward stragglers.

However, in the Middle East, some shepherds walk before the sheep and call them with a peculiar cry. It is this cry rather than simply voice recognition that guides the sheep.

Sheep in general are not very powerful, hence unable to defend themselves effectively. Moreover, they are not very good at recognizing localities, which explains why they can so easily go astray. When lost, the sheep panics. It falls to the ground and bleats loudly in hopes that it will attract the shepherd.

All this information and imagery is familiar and clear to the disciples, but they fail to grasp the point Jesus wants to make. Who is the honorable person and who is the thief, bandit, and stranger? He must explain it to them.

THE APPLICATION

At the implicit level, Jesus seems to be attacking the Jerusalem priests and the Pharisees. Leading sheep in and out echoes the symbolic description of Joshua in Numbers 27:16-17. Moses is urged to "appoint someone over the congregation who shall go out before them and come in before them, who shall lead them out and bring them in, so that the congregation of the Lord may not be like sheep without a shepherd." The leaders of Jesus' time are not doing this (see Mark 6:34).

At the explicit level, Jesus identifies himself as the gate. This image, however, is interpreted in two senses. In verse 8, Jesus notes that any *shepherd* who approaches the sheep other than through him (the gate) is a thief and bandit. In verses 9-10, Jesus is the gate through which the *sheep* must pass to gain life, salvation. This interpretation fits the parable in verses 1-3a rather clumsily; it must have been torn from a different setting (Ps 118:20; see John 14:6).

To find pasture is to find life. Sheep who seek pasture through Jesus find life, life in abundance (v. 10). The thief can offer only theft, destruction, and death. Such a shepherd contrasts starkly with Jesus the gate and the noble shepherd, the figure to which Jesus turns attention in the subsequent section.

If contemporary American believers can see beyond the sheep imagery to the question of leadership in the Christian community, today's few verses should stimulate healthy reflection. Are contemporary leaders noble guides or more like thieves, bandits, and strangers?

Fifth Sunday of Easter
John 14:1-12

FAREWELL ADDRESSES

Scholars identify chapters 14–17 of John's Gospel as the evangelist's creative presentation of teachings of Jesus in the form of a "farewell address."

The Bible reports farewell addresses from Jacob (Gen 49), Moses (Deut 31–33), Paul (Acts 20), and Jesus (Luke 22; John 14–17), among others.

In general, these passages begin with an indication that the speaker is about to die or depart. Then follows an exhortation to his successors. The elements in this part of the address vary: there are prophecies, words of caution about the future, God's intentions for the future. Successors are also exhorted to pass these words on to others. Sometimes there is also notice of the speaker's death and burial.

When John 14 concludes with "Rise, let us be on our way," we are surprised to see that John 15 continues the farewell address. Clearly the evangelist has strung together otherwise separate traditions.

What final advice does Jesus give in this part of his farewell address? It can be summarized in John Dominic Crossan's translation of verse 6: "I am the authentic (truth) vision (way) of existence (life)."

Jesus announces his imminent departure and return to take his disciples with him to a place of permanent fellowship with God. And he reminds them: "You know the way to the place where I am going."

Thomas, true to form, claims he doesn't know the way! It is in response to this that Jesus points to himself as the way, the only way in which human beings can meet God.

JESUS THE WAY

Jesus' words and deeds in this Gospel speak love at every turn. He demonstrates absolute, total, and universal love in his varied responses to those who approach him. Jesus' life, teaching, and behavior do indeed present people with "an authentic vision of human existence," that is, a model of the way human life ought to be lived. If one lives like this, one will definitely encounter God, who is Love.

These are heartening words not only to Jesus' disciples but especially to believers within John's community who are beginning to suffer for believing in Jesus. "The Judeans had already agreed that anyone who confessed Jesus to be the Messiah would be put out of the synagogue" (John 9:22; see also 12:42; 16:2).

Such excommunication deprived these people of a community and a place that were dear to them. Moreover it raised doubts about whether they really could meet God anywhere else. The synagogue, after all, represented God's chosen community. Jesus assures his disciples and through them all subsequent generations of believers: "If you know me, you will know my Father also." If one has met Jesus, one has met the Father.

Philip still doesn't get it. He asks Jesus to "show us the Father" (v. 8). This must have been particularly disappointing to the historical, earthly Jesus. Jesus himself called Philip to be a follower, and he in turn brought Nathanael to Jesus (John 1:43-48). When faced with a hungry multitude, Jesus turned to Philip and asked him how they could be fed (John 6:5-9). When curious Greeks wanted to meet and talk with Jesus, they approached Philip to intercede on their behalf (John 12:20-22). Only against this background can one appreciate Jesus' disappointment: "You still do not know me!?"

Philip's failure provides Jesus with the opportunity to point to the future successes of his followers: "The one who believes in me will also do the works that I do and, in fact, will do greater works than these . . ." (v. 12).

The works of Jesus are the works of God: to give life, and to restore meaning to life or enrich life's meaning. Already at creation God called us to take dominion over evolution ("to till the garden and keep it," Gen 1:26-28).

This is our challenge to engage in life-giving activities rather than death-dealing ones. This is also our challenge to put meaning into life rather than suck it out. This is what Jesus in his "last will and testament" urges his followers to do out of love for others.

Jesus has presented himself as the authentic vision of existence. Believers can only echo Peter: "Lord, to whom can we go? You have the words of eternal life" (6:68).

Sixth Sunday of Easter
John 14:15-21

REPETITION AND STYLE

Today's gospel concludes Jesus' response to Philip's request: "Show us the Father" (14:8). The beginning and end of this passage repeat the same idea but in reverse: "if you love me, you will keep my commandments" (v. 15) and "those who have my commandments and keep them are those who love me" (v. 21). Such a literary construction is called an "inclusion" characterized by "reverse parallelism." The text "included" within these verses is intended to be viewed as a unit.

The unit (vv. 16-20) contains three basic ideas, also repeated in parallelism.

(1) The Spirit is coming to the community as advocate, helper, counselor (v. 16); Jesus is returning (v. 18). This pattern repeats itself throughout the farewell address. Jesus alternates the expressions "I go to send the Spirit" with "I myself shall return." One and the same basic fact, that God does not abandon the community but remains ever with it, is captured in each statement.

(2) The forces of evil neither see nor know the Spirit (v. 17a); the disciples see the risen Jesus, source of their life (v. 19a). Seeing and failing to see are major themes in John's Gospel. Here the forces of evil (the world) stand in contrast to the force of Risen Life (the disciples).

(3) The disciples know the Spirit because he abides with and in them (v. 17b); the forces of evil do not see the risen Jesus, but the disciples recognize his abiding presence in the mutual love that they express freely and openly (vv. 19b-20).

A number of insights from Mediterranean culture help modern believers to gain a better understanding of John's repetitive style.

REPETITION AND MEANING

First, secrecy, lying, and deception are key strategies in this culture for protecting one's honor. It is always difficult to know the truth; the suspicion is always that others are lying. Though this makes life very difficult, the culture offers strategies for affirming that truth is being told. One is to call God to witness to what one says. The prohibition against using God's name in vain is a prohibition against calling God to witness a lie. The fact that such a commandment exists suggests that it was a common practice to name God as witness to a lie.

Other strategies for certifying truth involve statements such as "May God do thus and so to me if I speak not the truth," or "As I live" (meaning "I'm not lying"), or in John's Gospel Jesus' repeated affirmation "Amen, Amen," which some translations more appropriately render "Truly, Truly I say to you. . . ." Even Jesus had to assure others he was not deceiving them or lying.

Modern Western culture's access to polygraph tests, sodium pentathol, and similar means makes it difficult to appreciate the frustration the ancients felt in trying to discover the truth. Jesus' guarantee of the Spirit of truth as Paraclete was good news indeed.

Second, modern believers may feel uncomfortable about the contrasts John regularly draws between "us" (believers) and "them" (the world, the forces of evil). If John and his community sound slightly paranoid, that judgment may be more than partly correct.

Middle Eastern culture is agonistic, that is, it is conflict-prone. Its basic social institution is the large and very extended family. Everyone outside the family is suspected of being an enemy, plotting evil against the family, seeking to damage it. Truth was owed only to family and kin extending no further than the village. No one outside the village had a right to know anything.

This cultural orientation is challenged by Jesus' teaching to love one another and imitate the love that exists between Jesus and the Father. Jesus' love-command extends beyond the family and the village.

John's reference to "the world" or the forces of evil no doubt stems from this basic cultural hostility toward non-kin, but it also is based on the realization that some people refused to believe in Jesus and his message and sometimes did take hostile action (e.g., ejecting folks from the synagogue).

Since they live in a different culture, what role do Americans expect the Paraclete to play in their lives?

Seventh Sunday of Easter
John 17:1-11

THE MEANING AND TYPES OF PRAYER

Jesus ends his farewell address with two prayers (17:1-19, 20-26). The first is concerned with Jesus' immediate disciples after his death; the second looks to believers yet to come.

From a purely cultural perspective, prayer is a socially meaningful act of communication directed to persons perceived to be in control of the life situation of the one praying and performed for the purpose of getting results.

The message of the prayer reveals how the persons praying perceive themselves and God. This is captured in a traditional saying: *lex orandi, lex credendi,* that is, how and what we pray reveal what we believe about the one to whom we pray.

Prayer can address seven practical purposes. It can be: (1) instrumental ("I/we want"); (2) regulatory ("do as I/we tell you"); (3) interactional ("me/we and you"); (4) self-focused ("here I am/we are"); (5) heuristic ("tell me/us why"); (6) imaginative ("let's pretend"); and (7) informative ("I have something to tell you").

John 17:1-5. The first five verses of Jesus' prayer focus on the core Mediterranean cultural value, honor. The key word is "glory" or "glorify." Recalling that honor is a claim to worth *and* a public acknowledgement of that claim, we note that Jesus is praying in the presence of the disciples (and not in secret, as he once instructed them; see Matt 6:5-6).

Jesus' life-work, about to be culminated in his obedient death and resurrection ("the hour has come"), is his public claim to honor. Jesus has manifested the Father to the world and has provided human beings with the potential for authentic existence, eternal life in communion with God who has shown in Jesus that the divine nature is limitless love. Thus, only the Father can validate and confirm Jesus' claim to honor. The Father can affirm and demonstrate the preexistent honor that Jesus and the Father shared.

This portion of Jesus' prayer is instrumental, that is, it is a prayer to obtain a good (honor) and a service (public proclamation) from God to satisfy Jesus' and his disciples' social need: to be recognized as honorable people.

John 17:6-8. This portion of Jesus' prayer is self-focused, that is, he identifies himself and his disciples to God, with special emphasis on the disciples.

Jesus reminds the Father of their mutual relationship. The Father entrusted these creatures to him, and he in turn made the Father known to them. Through Jesus they have come to know the Father and the Father's will (word/words), and they recognize that Jesus was sent to them by the Father.

John 17:9-11. Jesus now switches the focus of his prayer back to the instrumental mode. He asks the Father "to protect them in your name that you have given me, so that they may be one, as we are one" (v. 11). This is a petition for unity in community. The reason for petitioning this protection for his disciples is that Jesus is taking leave of them.

Some self-focused dimensions of prayer enter into this section, too. Note how Jesus reminds the Father to distinguish between "those whom you gave me from the world" and "the world" of the forces of evil and rejection of God. It is precisely because Jesus must leave his chosen ones in this hostile environment that he pleads with the Father to continue to watch over and protect them.

What he expresses here in prayer, Jesus later accomplishes in deed when, dying on the cross, he entrusts his mother to the care and protection of a good friend.

Modern Western believers may consider this approach to Jesus' prayer as esoteric. But careful reflection on Western styles of public prayer reveals that very often these are composed with greater concern to impress or edify the human listeners than to stir God to action. The reason for this is that

Westerners are convinced that they are masters of their own destiny and are expected to look out for themselves. No one else will.

Our Middle Eastern ancestors in the faith believed that they had no control over their lives. Only God did, and public prayer stirred God to act because it put God's honor on the line. That was Jesus' intent in this prayer. How do American believers pray?

Pentecost
John 20:19-23

The change from "Holy *Ghost*" to "Holy *Spirit*" in the English translations of sacred texts was literally correct and long overdue. (Other languages always translated the original Hebrew and Greek words with "spirit.") Middle Eastern culture sheds significant light on the evolution of the meaning of these Hebrew and Latin words.

WIND AND POWER

The Hebrew word *ruah*, the Greek *pneuma*, and the Latin *spiritus* all basically mean "air in motion," "breath," or "wind." The root meaning is power. Apart from human and animal power, wind was the main observable energy source in the ancient world. Sometimes it was experienced as a cool, refreshing breeze (Gen 3:8), other times as a strong wind (Exod 10:13, 19), and sometimes it had hurricane or tornado force (1 Kgs 19:11).

Poetic texts in ancient literature frequently preserve archaic expressions. Thus, Psalm 18:15 (also 2 Sam 22:16) describes the wind as God's breath. "Then the channels of the sea were seen, and the foundations of the world were laid bare at your rebuke, O Lord, at the blast of the breath of your nostrils" (see also Exod 15:8; 2 Sam 22:16; Hos 13:15; Isa 30:28; Job 4:9). Thus, the primitive understanding of wind in the Bible is as the breath of a very powerful being.

WIND AS LIQUID

Also interesting is the ancient understanding of wind (and water and fire) as possessing what we now consider to be the properties of liquids. This explains why the ancients believed that the wind or spirit could be "poured out": "And I will never again hide my face from them, when I pour out my spirit upon the house of Israel, says the Lord God" (Ezek 39:29; see also Isa 32:15; Joel 3:1ff.).

WIND, GOD'S BREATH

Since human beings tend to perceive and understand God from a human perspective, our ancestors in the faith spoke anthropomorphically of God's arm (Isa 40:15), hand (Deut 2:15), face (Gen 33:10), mouth (Ps 33:6), and breath (Job 32:9; 33:4), which they understood to be God's vital power or spirit.

The Old Testament never presents the spirit of God as a person but rather as the power by which God acts in human life. This power is no more distinct or separate from God than a hand or mouth. Even so, God's power or breath acts outside of God and can be "sent" (Isa 48:16), "placed" (Isa 63:11), or "poured."

THE HOLY WIND, BREATH, SPIRIT

Later Judaism (Sirach, Daniel, Testament of Levi, Henoch, Esdras, Ascension of Moses, Sibylline Oracles) also generally refers to "the holy spirit" as divine power and not as a distinct person. It is first in the New Testament that the concept begins to become personified, even though Old Testament understandings still continue.

Thus, on the day of Pentecost, those gathered in the upper room heard a sound "like the rush of a violent wind" that filled the house (Acts 2:1-4). Luke describes the appearance of this wind as "divided *tongues,* as of fire," because the empowerment bestowed by this wind was the ability to "speak in other languages." Of course, God is the force or power behind this phenomenon attributed to his Spirit or breath.

This background helps a modern believer to appreciate what the apostles and Jesus understood to be taking place in today's gospel. Jesus announces that he is sending the apostles just as the Father sent him. Then he "breathes" on the Eleven (v. 22), imitating the moment of creation when God "blew" up the nostrils of Adam and brought him to life (Gen 2:7). The risen Jesus re-creates these human beings as children of God. "Receive a holy spirit," continues Jesus as he empowers the apostles to forgive and hold sins. The Greek word for "sin" here *(hamartia)* portrays it as an "evil power or force." (Twenty-five of the thirty-one occurrences of this word in John are in the singular!) Thus Jesus gives the apostles a holy power to fight against an evil power, a mighty force to do combat with an evil force.

John's viewpoint challenges modern believers to look beyond "lists of sins" and "new sins" and to view sin as an evil force. The good news is that Christ gives the spirit (or force) to all Christians to do battle against this evil force.

Trinity
John 3:16-18

"THE WORLD"–GOOD OR BAD?

Bumper stickers and personalized license plates inscribed "John 3:16" are a common sight on highways across the United States. One can only wonder if the contemporary Christian who proudly broadcasts this heart-warming message ("For God so loved the world . . .") realizes that it reflects only one phase in the life, loves, and hates of the first-century Johannine community.

John's Gospel expresses both a positive and negative attitude toward the "world." The positive attitude is clear in today's passage and elsewhere in the Gospel (1:29; 4:42; 6:33, 51; 10:36; 12:47; 17:21). Jesus is actually glad to "come into the world" (6:32; 11:27). He is the "light of this world" (8:12; 9:5; 12:46) who willingly became human and pitched his tent among us (1:14).

The negative attitude is actually more common. The world refused to receive Jesus (1:9-10) and is basically at odds with him (16:20; 17:14, 16; 18:36) and his Spirit (14:17; 16:8-11). In fact, the world positively hates Jesus and his followers (7:7; 15:18-19; 16:20).

In response, Jesus determines to judge the world (9:39; 12:31) because the sons of darkness live in it (12:35-36). He prosecutes the world as its judge (8:21-29). Later, the Paraclete will carry on the formal trial and convict the world of false righteousness, false judgment, and submission to the devil (16:8-11).

How are we to understand the mixture of these positive and negative attitudes and the coexistence of strong love and deep-rooted hatred in John's community long after Jesus departed this world? From a historical perspective, scholars acknowledge that John's community went through stages of development. In its earliest stage (mid 50s), this community saw the world as a good place but in need of reform. It needed and deserved evangelization. For the most part, Mediterranean Judean believers in Jesus attracted other Mediterranean Judeans to believe in Jesus.

At a slightly later stage (late 80s), some Judean audiences began to turn a deaf ear to the preaching and soon took measures to eject fellow believers in Jesus from the synagogues. This shocking experience stimulated the development of the negative attitude toward the "world."

In John's Gospel, chapters 5–12 indicate that the resistant and unbelieving "world" involves "some hostile and disbelieving Judeans." But chapters 14–17 reflect the period after the break between early Christians and the synagogue. At the same time, some of the Gentiles who joined the community began to disbelieve its claims. They were also included in this negative perception of "the world."

THE WAYS OF AN ANTISOCIAL GROUP

A cultural perspective sheds yet additional light on our Johannine ancestors in the faith. The shock of "excommunication" transformed John's community into an "antisocial group." This technical term describes a group that sets itself up in a society as a conscious alternative to the larger society.

Social scientists observe that this posture is always transitional (even if the transition takes a couple of hundred years). This group's use of the word "the world" (seventy-nine times in John compared to nine times in Matthew and three times each in Luke and Mark) is a clear indicator of the "us" versus "them" mentality.

One strategy of an antisocial group is to use the same language as the group against which it protests but to completely reverse it. American teens offer a modern example (e.g., "bad" really means "good"). John's Jesus revels in verbal displays such as punning and word play. His statements are frequently ambiguous, misunderstood, and in need of clarification. The fuller context of today's passage, Jesus' discussion with Nicodemus, reflects Jesus' deliberate play on the Greek word *anothen*, which means both "from above" and "again." Can one blame Nicodemus for misunderstanding?

Such peculiar use of language characterizes all antisocial groups. This strategy sharply separates the group from larger society but binds the group members into tight-knit relationships among themselves and with their founder. John uses a wide variety of synonyms to encourage and express this bonding: believing in Jesus, following him, abiding in him, loving him, keeping his word, etc.

As the Johannine scholar Raymond Brown notes, such activity can persuade believers to retreat from "the world" into their warm cocoon of life or inspire them to go forth and evangelize "the world." He criticizes the former as a "fortress mentality" but warns that the latter is a "naive" view. All believers must come to grips with disagreement and rejection and devise constructive rather than self-defeating responses to both.

Corpus Christi
John 6:51-58

Christians living in the twentieth century are heirs of a richly complex and refined tradition. Contemporary understanding of the Eucharist frequently clouds our vision of the challenges faced by our first-century ancestors in the faith and the strategies they employed to meet these challenges.

JESUS' HOMILY

Today's passage reports that Jesus' comments led his contemporaries to a violent dispute among themselves: "How can he give us his flesh to eat?" (v. 52). No one interpreted this statement literally. The violent dispute erupts because Jesus once again resorts to "anti-language" (see the commentary for Trinity Sunday). He uses familiar words like "manna," "bread come down from heaven," and "I am . . ." and creates new and jarring meanings. What was he really saying?

One clue is found in the verse that immediately follows today's reading: "Jesus said these things while he was teaching in the synagogue at Capernaum" (v. 59). It may be best to interpret today's passage as part of a "midrashic homily" Jesus preached in the synagogue. (The Hebrew word *midrash* means interpretation or explanation.)

Homilies by definition always explain biblical texts and apply them to life. A homily never was and should not now be a sermon or a speech or a lecture. What biblical text was Jesus explaining? This is not an easy question to answer.

We know that first-century Judeans read the Torah (the first five books of the Bible) in the synagogue. It was divided

94

into 150 sections which were read sequentially over a three-year period. A second reading, called the Haphtarah, was drawn from the Prophets. Some scholars hypothesize that a third reading came from the 150 canonical psalms. No one has yet discovered this "lectionary," but Aileen Guilding has attempted to reconstruct it. Nearly all scholars disagree with her reconstruction, but most if not all agree with her basic idea. If the lectionary could be reconstructed, we might have some idea of the text upon which Jesus was commenting in the synagogue at that Passover season.

THE TARGUMIM

This search would be a purely creative-imaginative exercise were it not for yet another ancient body of Jewish literature known as the Targumim (singular: Targum), which are paraphrases of the Hebrew Scriptures in the Aramaic language.

During the Babylonian Exile Israel gradually forgot its Hebrew language and adopted the language the Babylonians spoke: Aramaic or Chaldean. They could no longer understand the Hebrew Scriptures when these were read to them.

In the synagogues, therefore, one person would read from the Hebrew text while another person would translate, on the spot, into Aramaic. Gradually the translations became paraphrases, and in some instances the paraphrases became much longer than the text. By the sixth and seventh centuries C.E., two collections of such Targumim existed: the Babylonian and the Palestinian. The former in general is more literal, the latter more paraphrastic. In either case, scholars use great care in relying on these documents. Even though they were collected in the sixth and seventh centuries, they do contain concepts that reach back to the time of Jesus.

After extensive research, Bruce Malina concluded that the sermon in John's text appears to reflect a Palestinian Targum to Joshua 5:5–6:1 (the Haphtarah or second synagogue reading) which appears to have been linked with a first, Torah reading of Numbers 21:6-9. Both deal with the Exodus and the manna tradition.

John (or Jesus) appears to have utilized this manna tradition to explain how Jesus personally surpassed the deficiencies of manna. In other words, instead of following the Jewish tradition of explaining the Bible by the Bible, John (or Jesus) explains the Bible (the manna tradition) in the light of Jesus. This could and did provoke violent dispute. Not all would have agreed that Jesus is the fulfillment of and substitute for the Torah, the living word of God. Certainly "the world" didn't.

While many modern believers might insist that Scripture should not be so challenging to understand and interpret, this small excursion into our biblical tradition shows how much more there is to learn. What does the Eucharist and its relationship to manna mean to you?

Eleventh Sunday in Ordinary Time
Matthew 9:36–10:8

FACTIONS

Believers traditionally are content to call the group of Twelve whom Jesus selected "apostles." The social sciences distinguish groups with greater precision and offer additional insight into the nature of Jesus' group.

Technically speaking, the Twelve whom Jesus gathered around himself form a special kind of *coalition* called a *faction*. A coalition is a group that gathers for a specific purpose over a limited time with no intention of being permanent. The key characteristic of a coalition is its many-sided network of relations directed toward the achievement of limited goals. In general, coalitions are informal, loosely knit, and elective groups. Joining a coalition does not mean one has to quit other more basic groups such as one's family. The fishing conglomerate that included the families of Jonah (with his sons Simon and Andrew) and Zebedee (with his sons John and James) along with their hired hands could be an example of a coalition.

A faction is a special type of coalition characterized by the charisma of a central person who gathers followers and maintains firm loyalty in his core group. Jesus initiates his faction with the call of Simon, Andrew, James, and John (Matt 4:18-22). In today's story, he rounds out the core group by selecting and naming Twelve.

Individual members have strong relationships with the central figure but less loyalty and concern for one another. Recall the bold request of John's and James' mother of Jesus, that he grant her sons special status in the faction (Matt 20:20-28). The other ten were understandably angry when they learned of this and likely wished they had beaten these brothers to the punch.

Peripheral members of the faction are only loosely connected to the group and often divide their loyalties with other factions and leaders. Judas, who was elected as part of the core group, may in reality have only given limited loyalty to Jesus, even though he held the common purse.

JESUS' FACTION AND ITS MISSION

Matthew's Jesus clearly specifies the limited goals of his faction: "Go nowhere among the Gentiles, and enter no town of the Samaritans, but go rather to the lost sheep of the house of Israel" (v. 5). Moreover, the Twelve proclaim the same message Jesus did at the outset of his career, a proclamation taken over from John the Baptist: "The kingdom of heaven has come near" (v. 7; 4:17; 3:2).

At the same time, Jesus raises the status of his core group of followers by empowering them to heal and cast out demons. Effectively, Jesus promotes his core group to a position like his. He makes them brokers of God's power over spirits and disease. God alone has power to heal and exorcise. Human beings who share in this power must recognize it is God's and not their own possession.

This is the context for understanding the concluding verse of today's reading: "You received without payment; give without payment." Actually, in the Middle Eastern world there never was and still is no free gift. Every gift has strings attached. It expects repayment.

In the verses that immediately follow this reading, Jesus advises his apostles to take no gold, silver, copper, etc. They were to rely on hospitality, that is, kindness extended to strangers. If they receive this hospitality, they will evangelize; if not, they will move on.

The charge to the disciples that they "give without payment" is a prohibition to expect or demand anything over and above normal Mediterranean hospitality. When at home, disciples could rely on their families to take care of them. When on the road, they are to rely on hospitality. Making a living in this world is not the gathering of gold or silver, but initiating, cultivating, and maintaining a network of friends.

One final cultural note. Travel in the ancient Middle East was relatively rare. One stayed put. Moreover, travel was possible only in the dry season. Not only were roads manageable, but people were out and about waiting for crops to mature, watching the vineyards, tending flocks, etc. Jesus sends his "fishers of human beings" out when the fishing is best!

Contemporary believers fascinated by small groups among our group-oriented ancestors must remember that individualistic Americans join groups chiefly for personal reasons, for a very limited period of time, with low level of allegiance. From a social scientific perspective, the small group does not appear to be a good way to rejuvenate church life in America.

Twelfth Sunday in Ordinary Time
Matthew 10:26-33

SECRECY AND OPENNESS

For all practical purposes, there was no privacy in ancient village life. Everyone minded everybody else's business. Crowds followed Jesus even when he sought out deserted places (Matt 14:13). Village children were trained to spy out the secrets of other families while keeping the secrets of their own families intact.

The common suspicion in this society is that if one does not know what others are up to, they must be up to no good. They surely must be plotting something that would damage everyone in the village. Jesus chided his disciples for trying to keep the children away from him (Matt 19:13-15) because he didn't want to create the impression that he was trying to hide something.

Life in such a nosey world can be oppressive. Hence people resort to secrecy and deception in order to gain some breathing room. During the festival of Booths, Jesus' disciples urge him to go to Jerusalem and seek honor from the crowds. Jesus replies: "I am not going to the festival." Yet after his brothers had gone he also went, but in secret (John 7:10). This secrecy caused such confusion that the Jerusalem crowd was divided in their opinion about his reputation. Some said, "He is a good man," while others said, "No, he is deceiving the crowd" (John 7:12).

Given the prevalence of secrecy and deception in this society, how could one ever know when to believe another person? People resorted to various strategies to persuade others that they were indeed telling the truth. One strategy was to call God as witness. Ruth seeks to assure her mother-in-law, Naomi, that she truly intends to remain with her rather than return to her family by saying: "May the Lord do thus and so to me, and more as well, if even death parts me from you" (Ruth 1:17). The fact that one of the commandments prohibits summoning God to witness a lie ("You shall not make wrongful use of the name of the Lord your God . . ."; Exod 20:7) suggests that even oaths did not guarantee that truth was being told.

Jesus' oft-repeated phrase in John's Gospel, "Amen, Amen I say to you" (more appropriately translated "Truly, Truly I say to you") is echoed in the modern Middle East by the oft-repeated "Believe me!" The plea has a ring of exasperation in it.

Today's gospel is good news indeed: God the patron will uncover everything that is covered and will reveal all secrets (10:26). To enjoy these benefits, one had best acknowledge publicly that Jesus is God's favored broker (10:32).

GOD-GIVEN HONOR

Earlier in Matthew's Gospel (6:1-18), Jesus criticized the Pharisees who drew attention to their fasting, almsgiving, and praying in order to be seen by others and thereby to win honor from the crowds. Although the Pharisees behaved in culturally acceptable fashion, Jesus urges his disciple to do these same good deeds "in secret" (Matt 6:1-18).

With this advice, Jesus redefines honor, his culture's core value. Honor is a public claim to worth and a public acknowledgment of that claim. The Pharisaic almsgiving, prayer, and fasting behavior is normal and expected. Jesus teaches rather that honor bestowed by God is far superior to that which humans give. Do good deeds to win honor from God rather than from human beings!

Here is yet another example where Jesus' teaching is counter-structural rather than counter-cultural. He doesn't discard honor, which would be a counter-cultural move. Rather he retains honor but redefines it by showing that God determines what is truly honorable.

Americans cherish their privacy. They sue tabloid newspapers that invade it. They are shocked when they learn of the existence of storehouses of information gathered without their knowledge and consent about their spending habits, their financial situations, and the like. How would Americans respond to Jesus' good news that all secrets will someday be revealed?

Thirteenth Sunday in Ordinary Time
Matthew 10:37-42

THE BONDS OF FAMILY

Family (kinship) is the central social institution in the ancient Mediterranean world, just as economics is in our world. Jesus' requirement that his followers should love him more than they love mother, father, son, or daughter shocks his first-century listeners (v. 37). Here is some background to help a modern American appreciate the shock.

The ancient Middle Eastern family was very large and quite extended. It consisted of a father and all his children, including his married sons with their entire families, living in one place. The ideal marriage partner was a first cousin (one's father's brother's daughter), which bound this close-knit family together with even tighter bonds. The resultant mentality is "our family" against "everyone else."

To marry anyone other than a family member is unthinkable. To sever all family ties as did the "prodigal son" (Luke 15:11-32) is not only stupid but equivalent to suicide. Outside the family, no one can be trusted, no one will help you, as that renegade son quickly learned when his funds ran out.

The real consequences of leaving one's family are dire indeed. One not only gives up the basic claim to honor and status but also loses all of the family's economic, religious, educational, and social connections as well. Perhaps most disastrous of all consequences is loss of a connection to the land. These are all serious and life-threatening losses. They are what Jesus had in mind when he spoke of "taking up one's cross" and "losing one's life for my sake."

HOSPITALITY VS. FAMILY

Did he offer anything in exchange? Yes. He set up his own company of followers as a "replacement" family, a new gathering of people not linked by blood ties but by bonds of commitment to himself. This is clearly what Matthew portrays throughout his Gospel.

Specifically, Jesus reminds his Mediterranean listeners of another basic social institution in their culture intended to make up for separation from one's family, namely, hospitality. By definition, hospitality in the Middle East is extended almost exclusively by men almost exclusively to total strangers. (The care one extends to relatives is called "steadfast lovingkindness.")

Hospitality provides safe passage for families (like Abraham's, Gen 12) or smaller groups (like Lot's visitors, Gen 19) through regions where they have no kinfolk. Jesus exhorts new communities of followers to practice hospitality toward each other in order to make up for the loss of family advantage. Whereas in Middle Eastern culture the reward for hospitality was largely the honor that accrued to one who extended it, Jesus connects the practice of hospitality among nonrelated believers to a reward that God himself will give.

In the concluding verses of today's reading, the focus returns to missionaries (just as at the beginning of Matt 10). There is mention of a prophet, and a holy person, and others sent by Jesus on mission. Whoever receives them, receives Jesus as well and honors the Father who sent Jesus.

THE CHRISTIAN'S CONSOLATIONS

These exhortations are important because they offer at least two consolations. One consolation is for the consequences of leaving one's family of origin and transferring allegiance to the surrogate family now composed of nonrelated believers in Jesus. The other consolation is for the hardships encountered by followers of Jesus from Jewish competitors in their missionary work.

Americans may find these ideas just a little strange. American youngsters are socialized from an early age toward leaving the family of origin and setting up their own family, sometimes in a different city or state. The troubles a Mediterranean person experiences in leaving the family of origin have little resonance with modern believers.

Further, hospitality among Americans is reserved for family and other special people. A recent study of parishes in the United States discovered that generally speaking they were not very hospitable to newcomers and visitors.

Today's gospel challenges modern Western believers to reflect on two key ideas. What is the "real cost" of maintaining one's faith in Jesus? And how do Western believers relate to other believers, particularly those who appear unexpectedly in their midst, or those who are in special need?

Fourteenth Sunday in Ordinary Time
Matthew 11:25-30

GOD'S PATRONAGE

A literal translation of verse 27 in today's gospel makes its familiar proverb stand out with greater force: "No one knows a son except a father, and no one knows a father except a son and anyone to whom a son elects to disclose him." Our culture says, "Like father, like son."

Jesus reminds us that his Father is like a Mediterranean patron, a godfather. This is the meaning behind the title "Father, Lord of heaven and earth," which tells us that Jesus' Father is truly in charge of human existence, of all creation. Jesus is his broker, who mediates between the patron and the clients.

As everyone in the Mediterranean world knows, a patron is someone who freely selects clients and then decides to treat the clients "as if" they were family. Thus any image of father in the New Testament which does not entail the biological fact of parenthood ought to be properly understood in terms of patronage.

What is peculiar about this patron? Who are his "favorites"? Infants, but not literally: rather, the simple or powerless people, those unable to do or obtain anything for themselves. Children in the ancient Middle East were the weakest and most vulnerable members of society. About 30 percent died at birth or soon after. Thirty percent of live births died by the age of six. Sixty percent did not live past their sixteenth birthday. They had little status within the community or family, and until the age of maturity, the child was considered equal to a slave. In a famine, the elder would be fed before the children.

Jesus contrasts the "powerless" as primary objects of his Father's patronage with the "wise" and the "intelligent." These latter are much more capable of looking after their own destiny than infants might be. In fact, these people might have the wherewithal to be patrons themselves. It would be easy for them, like the greedy farmer with the bumper crop (Luke 12:16-21), to refuse to be patrons and hoard their surplus for their own purposes. Certainly one group of wise and intelligent people Jesus had in mind were the Pharisees.

THE EASY YOKE

This image provides Jesus with a natural segue to the topic of *yoke,* a word used metaphorically to describe those things that control the lives of people. Peasants always had a yoke. For the most part, their lives as tenant farmers were governed by the wills and whims of the landowners. Their lives as rustic folk whose subsistence means allowed them to live only from day to day were controlled by religious leaders who grew fat on tithes that they hoarded in the Temple instead of redistributing to the needy. In the village setting, Pharisees laid the yoke of their 613 commandments upon their followers and others who sought their advice about how to please God.

For all Israelites, reciting and living according to Deuteronomy 6:4ff.: "Hear, O Israel! The Lord is our God, the Lord alone. You shall love the Lord your God with all your heart . . ." was known as "bearing the yoke of the reign of God."

Having offered insight into the nature of God the patron as one who favors the powerless (infants), Jesus the broker invites his peasant listeners to "learn from me; I am your model."

Jesus' invitation echoes that offered by Wisdom in Sirach (51:23, 26): "Draw near to me, you who are uneducated, and lodge in the house of instruction. . . . Put your neck under her yoke, and let your souls receive instruction."

Jesus teaches and demonstrates a way of life, a yoke, that differs markedly from the one other Judean leaders taught.

He promises a yoke that is easy and a burden that is light (v. 30). The peasants found this enormously appealing.

Modern believers must realize that the Pharisees are not portrayed fairly in our Gospels. Still, no one would deny that their arrogance, pride, and playacting often cast a shadow on the wise instruction they offered.

Modern reformers and spiritual leaders could well take a lesson from Jesus' principal challengers. Spiritual elitism repels many more than it attracts. The best guides are those who practice what they preach.

Fifteenth Sunday in Ordinary Time
Matthew 13:1-23

Parables paint culture-based scenarios. Yet every one in the ancient world knew that the parable teller intended the scenario to refer to something more or something other than was described.

THE SOWER

In today's parable, the first question is, who is the sower? In the ancient world, sowing preceded plowing. Still, the manner of sowing described in this parable is sloppy and wasteful. If the sower is a landowner, the peasant audience would despise his waste of precious seed.

If the sower is a tenant farmer or a day laborer, the peasants would sympathize with his careful sowing which ends up wasting seed anyway because conditions are so difficult.

The impossibly extravagant harvest gives a clue to the identity of the sower. On average, one might expect a four- or fivefold return on sowing. Thirty-, sixty-, and a hundredfold boggle the imagination. If a wasteful landowner realized such a profit, Jesus' parable is hardly good news to the peasants who made up 95 percent of his audience. But if the sower were a peasant, then the good news is that the crop will satisfy the landowner, provide seed for next year's sowing, pay all taxes, and still leave enough for the peasant to feed the family.

Moreover, since it is clearly God and not human effort that produces this humongous harvest, the "something other" or "something more" that the parable intends is now very clear. The scenario describes sowing and farming, but it really points to a loving and provident God who looks after needy peasants.

INGROUPS AND CONFRONTATION

The parable reveals yet another dimension of peasant life in the first century. Jesus tells his disciples that parables are "ingroup" or "insider" language (see vv. 10-16).

Normally, one's ingroup consisted of one's household (including servants and slaves), extended family, and friends. All others, even in the same village, were the outgroup. Still, the shape of both groups was rather fluid and changed often. For instance, if a village came under attack from outsiders, the entire village banded together as a new ingroup.

Natives of the same village or quarter of a city who might be outgroup to each other at home become ingroup to each other when they find themselves in a remote location. That Jesus of Nazareth had a house in Capernaum (Mark 2:1), and that the first people from Capernaum whom he called to follow him responded so readily indicates the extent of Jesus' ingroup network at that place (Matt 4:18-22 and parallels).

In this conflict-oriented society, ingroups are ever in competition with one another. Familiar competing ingroups in the Gospels are the disciples of Jesus, the disciples of John the Baptist, the Pharisees, the Herodians, and the Sadducees, among others. Jesus' disciples accepted the invitation to "Follow me" in part because, like others in that society, they had some grievance against another ingroup and expected that Jesus' ingroup would redress that grievance.

In the larger picture, the entire "house of Israel" (Matt 10:6) was an ingroup despite the existence of many competing "sub-ingroups." The context of the commandment to "love one's neighbor" as oneself (Lev 19:18) defined neighbor as "your people" (v. 18) and "kin" (v. 17). Jesus' parable of the good Samaritan (Luke 10:29-37) seeks to answer a common question in the first century: Who belongs to the house of Israel?

Among outsiders, all of these ingroups that constituted the house of Israel were identified as "Judeans" (often erroneously translated as "Jews"). Judea, Perea, and Galilee were the geographic divisions of the house of Israel, but outsiders generally didn't keep these distinctions. What the residents of all three geographic divisions held in common was birth into the house of Israel and allegiance to the Jerusalem Temple.

All this discussion about ingroups and insider language is very jarring to modern believers who tend to hold Luke's idyllic view of the early followers of Jesus as living in loving harmony (Acts 2:42) and being constantly under attack by enemies. Hostility permeated this culture and colored everyone's behavior.

The difference between Americans and their Mediterranean ancestors in the faith is that Americans generally seek to avoid face-to-face confrontation. Hostility and competition takes place behind the scenes, out of sight.

In the final verses (18-23) of this reading, Matthew interprets Jesus' parable by identifying the seed as "the word of the kingdom" and exhorting people to hear, understand, and act upon the word. The challenge is quite familiar to American believers. It's not enough to "talk the talk," one must also "walk the walk."

Sixteenth Sunday in Ordinary Time
Matthew 13:24-43

ENEMIES AND RETALIATION

Experts describe Mediterranean society as *agonistic,* that is, hostile and conflict-oriented. Today's opening parable is an illustration of this feature.

An enemy has sowed weeds among the wheat. The fact is mentioned without comment. Jesus' audience understood this perfectly. Birth into a family means not only inheriting that family's honor status and its friends but also inheriting its enemies.

There are many reasons why families become enemies in the ancient world, but the consequences are always the same. A state of feuding develops and persists over a long period of time. One never knows but must always suspect that a feuding enemy is seeking to shame one's family.

In this story, the shame is planted soon after the wheat seeds are sown, but it does not become full-blown shame until the weeds have matured to the point where they are clearly distinguishable from the wheat. Now the entire village discovers the shame along with the landowner, and they begin to laugh.

The laughter grows even louder when the landowner instructs his servants to allow the weeds to grow alongside the wheat until harvest. The peasants expect retaliation and revenge. Instead, the landowner appears helpless and bested by his enemies. Before the invention of electricity and television, such feuds provided entertainment for the village. But appearances are deceiving. The landowner is shrewd as well as being a savvy farmer. He knows that the wheat is strong enough to tolerate the weeds' competition for nutrition and irrigation. After the harvest, the landowner will not only have grain for his barns, but extra, unanticipated fuel for his needs. Instead of shaming this landowner, the weed strategy has backfired and shamed the enemy. The landowner and his servants have the last laugh. The enemy bent on shaming others is shamed instead!

There is an interesting lesson here. Once again, Jesus' peasant audience recognized that this was not a lesson in agriculture. It may have been a lesson about cultural values. The "something other" or "something more" of this parable may well be the landowner's refusal to retaliate, to get even with the enemy. In a society dedicated to revenge, the landowner's victory by seeming to do nothing is a powerful lesson.

THE VINDICATION OF GOODNESS

As with the parable of the sower (Matt 13:1-23), Matthew provides an interpretation for the "ingroup" (see vv. 36-43). The explanation does not follow the scenario Jesus presented. Instead, every item in the story is given a different meaning. This process is known as *allegorization,* something the early Christians favored in their interpretation of Jesus' parables. This happened, in part, because many early Christians no longer shared the peasant world view or experience. Matthew's community may well have been city people with precious little appreciation for the fine points of farming.

Even so, the allegorical interpretation faithfully addresses other basic Mediterranean convictions, especially the overwhelming awareness by the majority of people that they had no control over their lives. They were at the mercy of otherworldly powers: God, the evil one, and the angels.

It was an everyday experience that the righteous often suffered and the wicked often prospered. The consolation for the righteous in these allegorically interpreted verses is that in the long run "God will get" the wicked, and "they'll get theirs" in hell. The righteous will "shine like the sun in the kingdom of their Father."

Modern Christian believers may find this amusing, but upon reflection they must admit that they don't have a much better solution for the wickedness in our midst. Even capital punishment does not appear to be a deterrent, and we face the same frustration as our ancestors in the faith.

The confidence of the landowner that his wheat will survive the effect of the weeds is worth pondering. A trust in goodness that is greater than the fear of wickedness could be a powerful weapon against rampant, senseless violence. It has worked before in history, and could work again if given a chance.

Seventeenth Sunday in Ordinary Time
Matthew 13:44-51

The series of images in these verses describing what God is like are drawn from the everyday experience of three non-elite groups in Jesus' world: farmers, merchants, and fishermen. The details behind each of these images are presupposed. Filling in the details reveals the complexity of these simple-sounding stories.

HIDDEN TREASURE

The very last words of this verse constitute the major problem: "[he] buys that field." As John Dominic Crossan has pointed out: "If the treasure belongs to the finder, buying the land is unnecessary. But, if the treasure does not belong to the finder, buying the land is unjust" *(Finding is the First Act)*.

Burying valuable objects was a common practice in antiquity. Retrieving them was also common. Forgetting about the treasure or dying without telling one's heirs or before being able to retrieve it are possible explanations for the finding of treasure by those who don't own it.

Rabbinic lore is filled with debates concerning how to determine whether the finder had a right to the find or not. The circumstances of Jesus' parable suggest that this man did not. Why else would he hide it again?

Remember that a parable always points to "something more" or "something other." The key word here is "joy." God or God's reign is the hidden treasure. To find God brings great joy, but the discovery has a potential for disaster as well as for grace. The finder's joy seems to have led him to disaster. He sells "all that he has." Given what we know of the difficulties of farming, such self-impoverishment to purchase a field courts disaster. The finder has nothing to fall back upon. Worse, he now owns a field with a buried treasure which he dare not dig up because it will raise questions about ownership of the treasure, the morality of buying the field, and the character of this "lucky" (!?) finder. (Recall that in a society like this one which believes that all goods are finite in quantity and already distributed, when someone suddenly has increased possessions, that increase must be explained.)

American folk wisdom would say: "Finders keepers, losers weepers," but modern Americans would be no less suspicious and critical of the finder in this parable than his own Middle Eastern contemporaries. The treasure of the kingdom can be both rewarding and potentially corrupting.

PRECIOUS PEARL

Here the merchant is at the center, someone accustomed to buying and selling. His discovery is not by accident but the result of a calculated search.

Yet he, too, sells all to acquire this great pearl. What will he live on now? Ultimately, he may have to sell the pearl. The merchant and the accidental finder reveal "something more" and "something other" about the kingdom, about God, in their respective scenarios. The potentially corrupting power of the kingdom is the desire to possess or hoard it.

THE NET

The straightforward story of fishermen sorting their catch is similar to the parable of the wheat and weeds. This parable too receives an interpretation in the Gospel. As in the earlier parable, here also supraworldly agents, the angels, make the final discrimination and see to the appropriate punishment for the wicked. The "bad" fish are either inedible inhabitants of the sea or unclean sea creatures (see Lev 11:10-12), that is, those fish and other creatures not having scales or fins.

Americans love stories, and Jesus' parables are probably the best-known segments of the New Testament among American Christians. Like some of their Christian ancestors, modern Americans like to make allegories of the parables, or recreate them and Jesus' world in the American image. In the concluding verses of today's reading, the disciples answer with a resounding yes when Jesus asks whether they have understood these parables. Of course they have. The parables are discourses for insiders or ingroups, and Jesus made it a point to explain his message to these insiders, his intimate followers. Like these insiders, Americans must strive to discover the "something more" and "something other" to which each parable points. Appreciating Jesus as a Middle Eastern storyteller can help.

Eighteenth Sunday in Ordinary Time
Matthew 14:13-21

Matthew has intentionally contrasted two "banquets": one hosted by Herod which resulted in the death of John the Baptist (Matt 14:1-12) and this feeding of a large crowd by Jesus near the shore of the Sea of Galilee (14:13-21). (Consult the reflection on Luke's version of this story in *The Cultural World of Jesus Sunday by Sunday,* Cycle C, "Corpus Christi," for additional information.)

Herod's banquet takes place in an environment of scheming and arrogance and concludes with a murder. Prior to feeding the crowd that was following him, Jesus felt compassion for their needs and healed their sick. Herod's banquet was held at a royal court. Jesus' meal with this crowd took place in a "deserted" place by the Sea of Galilee, yet close enough to villages for the crowd to purchase food. This phrase, "deserted place," reminds the reader of the wilderness where God fed Israel with the manna. Matthew takes every opportunity to link Jesus with Moses.

Contemporary, scientifically minded, rationalist American believers are skeptical about a multiplication of loaves. Some interpreters propose that the "miracle" was Jesus' success in getting this group of people to share their personal provisions. Such sharing would be truly extraordinary for an American crowd of individualists but quite commonplace in the group-oriented Mediterranean world.

There is no way for us to reconstruct this historical event, but there is sufficient evidence to confirm that it really happened. Cultural insights help complete Matthew's scenario.

THE SETTING

Jesus commands the crowd to sit down on the grass (v. 19), but Matthew does not mention the clusters or their size as do Mark and Luke. Since it is a public place, it is culturally inappropriate for men and women to be present together. They are separated: men and young boys in their place, and women, girls, and boys under the age of puberty in a separate place. (A photo in the October 1987 issue of *National Geographic* shows a Saudi family separated into gender groups relaxing by the Red Sea.)

THE FOOD

Matthew mentions five loaves of bread and two fish. John (6:9) specifies barley loaves, and this is plausible for Matthew's situation as well. Barley could be raised on soils of poorer quality and was less expensive (see Rev 6:6). Barley bread was the ordinary food of the peasant classes. Even so, peasants often mixed barley with other grains like millet, spelt, or pea meal in making bread (Ezek 4:9).

Since the crowd is gathered near the Sea of Galilee, the presence of fish is not surprising. During that biblical period when Israelite access to the Mediterranean was limited, fish had to be purchased (Neh 13:16). In the Hellenistic period (after 300 B.C.E.), fishing at the Sea of Galilee became a government-regulated activity which involved catching the fish, preparing, and distributing them. Fish became more common in the first-century diet.

Jerusalem had a "fish gate" (Neh 3:3). Bethsaida on the northern shore of the Sea of Galilee means "fishing village" (Mark 6:45). The Greek name for the town of Magdala on the western shore of the Sea of Galilee was Taricheae, which means "processed fish."

In addition to these stories of Jesus feeding the crowd with fish, the New Testament reports a son asking his father for a fish (Matt 7:10). And after his resurrection, Jesus eats broiled fish (Luke 24:42) and processed fish (John 21:13) with his disciples.

In John 6:9, the Greek word definitely describes fish already cooked, that is, processed for shipping and marketing. Fish were processed as cured, pickled, salted, or dried, and wine could sometimes be mixed in with the fish brine. The Greek word for fish used in Matthew suggests that these may have been fresh fish but it does not exclude the possibility of processed fish.

THE OUTCOME

All ate their fill, and there were leftovers as well. Matthew's final comment (which occurs only in his account) helps us to realize that this crowd was much larger than five thousand because this number did not include the women and children who ate apart from the men.

The Eucharistic coloring of this story is clear in Jesus' blessing, breaking, and giving the loaves. What do Mediterranean cultural insights contribute to the story? How has American culture influenced contemporary celebrations of the Eucharist?

Nineteenth Sunday in Ordinary Time
Matthew 14:22-33

FISHING

In 1986 the level of the Sea of Galilee was extraordinarily low. Marine archaeologists discovered an ancient fishing boat in mud along its northwest shore, a little north of ancient Magdala (modern Migdal).

Basing themselves on the type of construction, the pottery found nearby, and the results of a carbon 14 test, the experts concluded that the boat was built between 40 B.C.E. and 70 C.E. It is very likely the kind of boat mentioned in today's story, the one used by the Jonah-Zebedee fishing syndicate (see Luke 5:10), which included their sons Peter, Andrew, James, and John, and hired hands.

The government regulated the fishing industry by selling fishing rights to tax collectors or publicans (brokers). These contracted with fishermen and frequently had to capitalize them. Since Matthew the toll collector had his office in Capernaum (Matt 9:1, 9), an important fishing center, it is likely that he brokered the government's fishing rights to his fellow citizens.

The boat found in the mud was 26½ feet long, 7½ feet wide, and 4½ feet deep. Originally it had a sail. There are places for four oarsmen and a tillerman. A boat this size could hold a crew of five plus ten passengers (v. 22), or the crew plus cargo, for instance, a catch of fish in excess of one ton (Luke 5:4-11; John 21:1-14).

With this background, a modern reader can easily see that first-century Mediterranean fishermen were far from middle class. They were ever at the mercy of the brokers (toll collectors) who capitalized their fishing venture and to whom they were ever in debt. They had no control at all over their activities.

SPIRITS AND STORMS

The fishermen also realized that they had no control over nature. Even though they were very familiar with the Sea of Galilee, no one among them was capable of predicting the storms that broke out unexpectedly, almost suddenly. They were at the mercy of the sea to provide a livelihood, and in the case of a storm like this, to spare their lives.

Earlier in Matthew's story line (8:23-27), Jesus was asleep in the boat with his disciples when a violent storm broke. They had to wake him to plead for help! On that occasion Jesus "rebuked" the winds and the sea, and a dead calm ensued.

In today's story, Jesus is absent when a strong head wind raises high waves that batter the boat and frighten its passengers. When the disciples see Jesus, they think he is a "ghost." When Peter steps out of the boat to meet Jesus, he "sees" the strong wind.

Both stories reflect the first-century Mediterranean belief in spirits, including wind spirits, that play havoc with human life. The only remedy for a human being is to find a more powerful spirit to counter the annoying spirit. This, of course, is God and his broker, Jesus, who throughout the gospel displays power to control evil and mischievous spirits.

Both stories also emphasize that the disciples wavered in their loyalty to God. "Why are you afraid, you of little faith?" (8:26). "You [Peter] of little faith, why did you doubt?" (14:31). The biblical term "faith" is best rendered "loyalty." Patrons will never fail clients who are loyal to them.

PRAYER

Here and in Gethsemane (26:36ff.) are the only places where Matthew reports that Jesus prayed. What does it mean to pray? Prayer, from the Mediterranean cultural perspective, is a message communicated to someone who is ultimately in charge of one's existence. The purpose of prayer is always to get results.

While in Matthew 14:13 the crowd followed Jesus as he tried to steal away to pray alone, here in verse 23 he manages to go up the mountain and spend most of the night alone in prayer.

When Jesus comes to the disciples tossed about on the sea by the storm and stills the storm, we see the results of Jesus' prayer. God responds to Jesus' loyalty (faith) by calming the sea, just as God would have continued to support Peter's walk on water if Peter had remained loyal (had faith).

Today's gospel asks scientifically oriented and technologically proficient Americans where human beings ought to place their faith or loyalty: in themselves or in God?

Twentieth Sunday in Ordinary Time
Matthew 15:21-28

Three aspects of Mediterranean culture place this reading in a fresh perspective.

HONOR AND SHAME

When he sent the Twelve on mission, Jesus directed them to "the lost sheep of the house of Israel" and urged them to steer clear of the Gentiles and Samaritans (Matt 10:5-6). Now Jesus himself heads in pagan direction, toward Tyre and Sidon, and is met by a pagan (Canaanite) woman from that region (v. 21). Will he contradict himself? This would be a shameful reversal of his earlier honorable charge to the Twelve.

CHALLENGE AND RIPOSTE

Always keep in mind the very public dimension of life in the Middle East. There is always a crowd at hand to watch, judge, and decide whether to grant honor or impute shame. The Canaanite woman uses the crowd to her advantage and hurls a challenge at Jesus.

Like others in the gospel, she cleverly addresses Jesus with an honorific title: "Lord, Son of David," and uses this title as a basis for her request: "have mercy on me." In the Middle Eastern world, mercy is a sensitivity to and sense of responsibility for one's debts to God and other human beings. People who ask for mercy feel they are owed something; people who show mercy acknowledge and pay what they owe.

The woman's plea is based on recognizing Jesus' Davidic ancestry and hoping he will act in accord with the reputation of the great King David. He will offer a remedy, perhaps a cure, for her demon-tormented daughter. Jesus is not obliged to answer the challenge. The woman is a pagan, he is an Israelite. They are not equals, and the honor game can only be played by equals. Following the honor code of his culture, Jesus ignores her.

The woman is not put off. She continues to follow the crowd and shriek after Jesus and his disciples (v. 23). Her behavior undoubtedly attracts an even larger crowd. The disciples urge Jesus to send her away. Their suggestion is unclear: send the woman away by healing her daughter or without doing so? Jesus' answer seems to imply that the disciples meant the former. He continues to refuse by citing his commitment "only to the lost sheep of the house of Israel."

But the woman is not to be denied. She comes forward, kneels respectfully to honor Jesus, and again uses the honorific title, "Lord." This time her plea is simple and moving: "Help me."

Jesus responds harshly and argues against throwing the children's food to dogs. This is an enormous insult to the woman. Gentiles were commonly referred to as dogs. Jesus apparently repeats his culture's stereotype. Calling a woman a dog is offensive in every language. Jesus has no qualms.

To everyone's amazement, including Jesus, the woman retorts with cleverness: "Lord [note the honorific title], even dogs eat crumbs that fall from their master's table" (v. 27). The woman proves she can give as good as she gets. She is equal to the game of challenge and riposte. She is the only person in the Gospels who proves to be a good match for Jesus' wit.

The fact is not lost on Jesus. He responds with the equivalent of "touché!" and grants her request. The daughter is healed instantly.

FAITH

Western believers for a long time have intellectualized faith, sometimes equating it with conviction or knowledge.

In the Middle East, faith is best understood as loyalty and commitment to a person, "no matter what." The woman was committed to Jesus from the outset of this exchange and very likely even before she undertook to go and meet him in person. She was not put off by his initial aloofness, nor his subsequent gruffness and insult. She determined to be loyally committed to him no matter how crudely he behaved. In the Middle East, such loyalty and commitment pay off.

Americans have a different experience of loyalty. Recent economic experiences appear to indicate that it does not pay. Long-term employees are laid off with hardly an afterthought. Firms that used to treat employees like family now have no choice but to downsize their operation and release long-time faithful workers. When this happens in the Church, its effect is even worse. What can American believers do to reactivate loyal commitment to Jesus and his Church?

Twenty-First Sunday in Ordinary Time
Matthew 16:13-20

Today's familiar story takes on a very different orientation when placed respectfully in its Mediterranean cultural context.

DYADIC PERSONALITY

Americans are recognized as the most individualistic people who ever lived on the face of this planet. Each one strives to be distinct. In the United States, everyone has a personal social security number and many other distinctive and singular identities.

Mediterranean people are exactly the opposite. Experts describe them as dyadic personalities. The word *dyad* means "pair." Such people are other oriented to such an extent that they have no sense of their individuality but depend rather on the opinions of others to help them know who they are.

Jesus' question, therefore, is not a "theology quiz" for his disciples. It reflects a normal, Mediterranean curiosity by Jesus, a dyadic personality, about what other people think. Like everyone else in this culture, Jesus needs such feedback because he does not know who he is, and he is trying to learn this from significant others in his life.

STEREOTYPING

In Jesus' case, the question is particularly interesting because the normal stereotyping of that culture was not working. Jesus' enemies feel satisfied in knowing him as "Jesus of Nazareth."

To know a person's home village is to know everything about that person. All people in Nazareth were presumed to be alike. Nathanael's rhetorical question, "Can anything good come from Nazareth?" (John 1:46) simply echoes the commonly held, stereotypical image of that village's inhabitants: worthless or no good.

Another stereotypical identification of Jesus is "the stone worker's or wood worker's son" (Matt 13:55; Mark 6:3). The ancient wisdom observed, "like father, like son."

To know a family was to know everything about every member of that family. "'Is not his mother called Mary? And are not his brothers James and Joseph and Simon and Judas? And are not all his sisters with us? Where then did this man get all this?' And they took offense at Jesus" (Matt 13:55-57). One reason for the offense was that Jesus was not engaged in the same profession as Joseph, as a dutiful and respectful son should be. Jesus knew all these stereotypical identities that belonged to him. Still he asks Peter for his opinion.

True to Mediterranean form, Jesus' disciples tell him what others are saying about him, and how others are perceiving him: John the Baptist, Elijah, Jeremiah, another of the prophets. All of these are honorable if mistaken perceptions. But Jesus presses for Simon's opinion, and he says, "the Messiah, the son of the living God."

JESUS' IDENTITY

Jesus now has a rather large assortment of opinions to ponder. In gratitude to Simon for this information, Jesus bestows on him a nickname, Rocky or Peter. New names were regularly given at significant moments in a group's life, especially to the more prominent members. "Rocky" has played the role of a moral entrepreneur throughout the gospel, supporting Jesus' career from the day he answered his call and prodding it along at every opportunity. (Later, Peter's associates James and John would prod their mother to obtain a favor for them from Jesus, so that they might outstrip Peter and his new nickname. See Matt 20:20-28.)

In addition, Jesus promises that Peter will become like him, a broker who can provide access to God the patron. This is the significance of giving him the "keys of the kingdom." Keys open doors, which is another way to describe a broker's specialty.

Over and beyond that, Peter is given a distinctive power to declare authoritative judgments ("binding and loosing"), something which appears to have been given to all the disciples in Matthew 18:18.

If American believers read Jesus' question here from the intense psychological perspective that dominates modern American convictions about self-knowledge and knowledge of others, they will assume Jesus knows who he is and is testing his friends to see if they know. If they use the Mediterranean scenario painted above, they will have to assume Jesus does not know and looks to significant others in order to find out. How will you read the passage?

(For additional Mediterranean cultural insights and reflections on Luke's version of this same episode, see *The Cultural World of Jesus Sunday by Sunday*, Cycle C, "Twelfth Sunday in Ordinary Time.")

Twenty-Second Sunday in Ordinary Time
Matthew 16:21-27

The verse that immediately follows today's reading helps us better understand what preceded: "Truly I tell you, there are some standing here who will not taste death before they see the Son of Man coming in his kingdom" (Matt 16:28).

PRESENT ORIENTATION

Mediterranean people of antiquity and the present are primarily oriented toward the present. It is difficult and sometimes impossible for them to think "future." The best they could imagine would be called "forthcoming." The birth of a baby is a forthcoming event for an already pregnant mother. A harvest is a forthcoming event from a crop already planted and growing.

This perspective is starkly evident in Jesus' stated conviction that those who heard him speak would still be alive when God would bestow his gifts upon that very generation through the mediation of the Son of Man.

Jesus died, was raised, and ascended to the right hand of the Father. And still the Son of Man has not come in his kingdom. It is the long delay (now centuries old) that sparked a vague idea of a real "future" among some Mediterranean Christians.

PETER CHALLENGES JESUS

In his own lifetime, Jesus was able to read the handwriting on the wall. He had made an ever-growing number of powerful enemies. Their desire to have him put to death was no secret.

After learning from his disciples that others held him in high repute, ranking him along with Elijah, John the Baptist, and other worthies, Jesus could not turn away from the ominous destiny he began to perceive on his own horizon. But when he stated the obvious to his disciples, Peter took him aside and said he had other plans for Jesus. Peter and Jesus now engage in a common Middle Eastern strategy revolving around honor: challenge and riposte. One person makes a claim to honor, another person challenges that claim. The first person must defend or vindicate his claim or he will be dishonored, shamed.

Jesus' claim to honor is that God wills his suffering and death at the hands of his enemies (he *must* die), but that God will bestow even greater honor by raising him from the dead.

Peter's challenge is: "God forbid it" (v. 22). Jesus has just enunciated God's honorable will, and Peter seeks to divert Jesus from fulfilling it. He wants God to change it. Jesus perceives that Peter is testing his loyalty to God, his very claim to honor.

Jesus' riposte (a fencing term describing a sharp, swift thrust after parrying an opponent's lunge) is to call Peter a "satan," a tester of loyalties. Jesus continues the insult by reminding Peter that he sees only the human way of thinking and doesn't understand God's plan.

This scene echoes an earlier test of Jesus' loyalty to God. At Jesus' baptism, God declares him to be a "pleasing son" (Matt 3:17). Immediately, Jesus is driven by spirits into the desert where, after a forty-day fast, the devil tests his loyalty and tempts him to disobey God (the challenge). In each of the three tests, Jesus manages a deft riposte, quoting Scripture against the devil's scriptural attack.

TRUE HONOR

Verses 27-28 are yet another redefinition of honor. Clearly these verses describe reversal. What society considered honorable (avoiding the cross; saving life) is rejected. What society considered shameful (carrying the cross; losing life) is defined as honorable.

The statements are vague, yet there are similar exhortations in ancient literature. In the *Anabasis,* Xenophon noted that soldiers who try to preserve their lives in battle are shameful, but those who strive to die well will be better off, especially if they survive. John (15:13) notes how honorable it is to give one's life out of loyalty in friendship.

All these statements, vague as they may be, are typical of cultures where speech is more evocative than explicit. Jesus' exhortations shatter the normal cultural vision of an honorable life and invite his listeners to consider reorienting their lives by means of disorientation. A fitting message for anyone searching for new direction in life.

Twenty-Third Sunday in Ordinary Time
Matthew 18:15-20

Our ancestors in the faith and Mediterranean culture in general are prone to conflict. (The technical word is *agonistic,* deriving from the Greek for battle, struggle, contest.) From experience they know that conflict is dangerous because it can escalate to violence and result in bloodshed, starting a blood feud that wouldn't end until everyone was dead.

For this reason, they utilize a wide array of strategies to defuse conflict. One is to fume and threaten with no intention of ever carrying out the threat. Jesus fulminated against Chorazin, Bethsaida, and his "second" home village, Capernaum, but left it to God to settle accounts (Matt 11:20-24). Having vented his steam, he calmly recited a prayer of praise to the Father. The cultural belief is that words are better than action.

Another strategy for defusing conflict is to turn the other cheek rather than engage in tit for tat, or eye for eye (Matt 5:38-41). This strategy is not popular among Americans. Popular wisdom advises, "Don't get mad, get even," and the rising tide of violence in this country suggests that many citizens follow this cultural wisdom.

Today's gospel passage presents three more strategies for conflict resolution. The word "brother" (New American Bible translation) in Matthew's Gospel always means "another member of the church" (New Revised Standard Version). The advice is intended to head off conflicts between insiders; it is not intended to govern relationships with outsiders.

CONFRONTATION

The conflict arises because "sin" is an interpersonal offense. In societies where honor is the core value, it is very easy to sin against another, to offend another's honor. People learn from an early age the potentially fatal consequences of such an offense.

If someone thinks another person has shown dishonor, the offended party is advised to confront the sinner in private ("when the two of you are alone"). The reason for this privacy is to avoid placing the suspected offense within the official arena of honor and shame, that is, the public eye. If the perception of dishonor has been mistaken, or the alleged dishonor unintentional, the conflict has been successfully defused in private. No one has lost face.

NEGOTIATION

The second strategy is to take along two or three negotiators or witnesses (v. 16). Now the situation is semiprivate and becomes a legal matter (see Deut 17:1-7 which requires more than one witness). The Greek word in verse 19 translated as "anything" literally means "legal case, litigation." The witnesses are fully aware of the seriousness of their role (see Exod 20:16; Acts 6:13) and the consequences of bearing false witness (Deut 19:15-21). Whatever they decide is legally binding. The hope is that the negotiators or witnesses will succeed where individual efforts failed. Honor must be repaired or restored in order to avoid the next step.

ADJUDICATION

The final strategy now fully engages the cultural values of honor and shame. The matter is related to "the church," that is, the entire community. The event has become fully public and publicized. In matters of honor and shame, the community is the final arbiter. If the offender chooses to disregard the community's judgment, the consequence is excommunication. To be considered as "a Gentile and a tax collector" is to be designated an "outsider." The recalcitrant sinner is thrown out.

The force of excommunication is lost on American individualists who have little allegiance to any group, including family. Americans prefer to "go it alone" and "do it my way." "See if I care. I gotta be me!" Not so our Mediterranean ancestors in the faith. Without community one is effectively dead. One has no network, no support, no hope. And to be lumped with one's enemies is the worst of punishments.

THE JUDGMENT

The plural "you" in verse 18 means that all disciples of Jesus have authority to bind or loose, that is, to settle conflicts and legal cases between community members. When the community gathers in Jesus' name to hear a legal case, Jesus is there. When the community agrees, the Father in heaven agrees. How shameful a thing is conflict among Christians.

Twenty-Fourth Sunday in Ordinary Time
Matthew 18:21-35

Last week we reflected on sin as an interpersonal offense, something that divides members of the Christian community. When the sinner refuses to admit the sin, he or she is thrown out of community. When the sinner admits the sin, the community's forgiveness reinstates him or her to membership. Reconciliation ("forgiveness from the heart," v. 35) presumes and is based upon forgiveness.

Today's reading proposes two ideas. Central to each is how "members of the church" (see the NRSV translation) are to behave toward each other. The first idea in Jesus' reply to Peter's question is that disciples of Jesus must forgive one another always ("seventy times seven"), without limit. The second idea, found in the parable, is the communal dimension of forgiveness.

Let us take a closer look at the parable (vv. 23-35).

DEBTS

First-century Mediterranean peasants understood sin, that is, interpersonal transgressions, after the fashion of debts. That is what Jesus taught his followers to ask of God: "Forgive us our debts, as we also have forgiven our debtors" (Matt 6:12). For Westerners accustomed to a money-driven economy, debts almost always translate into "money owed." Since economics is our culture's predominant institution, everything is viewed from an economic perspective. In drug arrests we hear not of people saved from potential addiction, but rather the dollar value of the drugs confiscated. In natural disasters we hear not so much of people's misfortunes but rather the economic loss in terms of dollars.

Not so our peasant ancestors, for theirs was not a money-based economy. Their lives were based on interpersonal relationships even in what we would recognize as "economic" transactions. In such a culture, the purpose of haggling is not economic but interpersonal. That the potential buyer will make a purchase is a foregone conclusion. The buyer haggles and the seller willingly goes along because both are building an interpersonal relationship called friendship (see Gen 18:22-33; Jas 2:23). Friends will be faithful: the seller will always set and the buyer will always get a good price.

In fact, the seller feels obliged to sell at a lower price to people of lower status, and at a higher price to people of higher status and one-time customers. Add the uncertainty of this style of business management to the variety of taxes (as much as 35 to 40 percent of peasant agricultural production) a seller had to pay, and it is easy to see why the peasant was very familiar with debt.

THE PARABLE

Everyone in the parable belongs to one big household, "as if family." In taking account of his household, the king learns one slave owes him an impossible amount. (A talent was equivalent to 6,000 denarii; a denarius was approximately one day's wage. Ten thousand talents would require more than 164,000 years of work, seven days a week.)

But the king is sensitive to his honorable reputation. If he deals harshly with a servant of his own household, his subjects will judge him to be shameless, a man without honor. So the king decides to act in "mercy" and forgive the debt. He gains more honor by this decision than he would by insisting on receiving full payment of the debt.

In behavior that is both shocking and sad, the forgiven slave turns toward a fellow slave in the same household and refuses to forgive a much smaller debt. He refuses to imitate the merciful behavior of the king-patron. If he gets away with this strategy, the king will become a laughing stock. To protect his honor, the king-patron has no choice but to put this brazen slave in his proper place: jail!

The moral of Jesus' story is that members of the community must treat one another as God has treated each of them. They must choose the more honorable path and forgive one another "from the heart." Jesus' instruction echoes Leviticus 19:17: "You shall not hate your brother in your heart . . . you shall love your neighbor [understood here as a fellow-Israelite, a member of your in-group] as yourself." How well do Americans fare on forgiving or loving each other from the heart?

Twenty-Fifth Sunday in Ordinary Time
Matthew 20:1-16

What is God like? The answer to this common question always reflects the culture of the questioner or the one who answers the question. Today's parable reports one of Jesus' many answers to this question. It should be no surprise that in this parable God behaves in accord with Middle Eastern values.

LIMITED GOOD

In general, Americans believe that "there is always more where this came from," whether it is oil, jobs, money, or whatever. This attitude makes it extremely difficult for Americans to understand concepts such as shortages, extinction, or anything similar.

Our Mediterranean ancestors in the faith believed "there is no more where this came from." Everything (jobs, wealth, honor, or whatever one could imagine) was limited in quantity and already distributed. The jobs at the vineyard were already filled. How dare any worker think there might be more jobs?

Moreover, to ask for a job is to deprive the employer of something he owns. This is shameful. Instead, workers have to be invited by the owner to work for him. The owner in this parable goes out five times in one day looking for workers to invite, and each time he hires everyone in sight. Such behavior by the owner and the potential workers is very honorable, because it respects the cultural idea that all goods—including jobs—are limited.

PATRONAGE

In America, workers look for jobs, employers hire the best qualified workers, they agree on a wage and respect a practice called "seniority." None of this existed in the ancient Mediterranean world and none of these elements can be found in the parable.

Only to the first hired does the owner promise "the usual daily wage." They agree to accept it. To the second (and presumably all subsequent groups), the owner says: "I will pay you whatever is right."

At the end of the day, the owner pays the workers beginning with the last hired. This is an important narrative point without which the story would collapse because those hired first would have no reason to hang around if they were paid first. This point also indicated to ancient Mediterranean peoples that the owner wears two hats: he is an employer but can also be a patron.

A patron is a person of means who freely chooses to treat other people (always of lower status) "as if" they were family members. No one can bid for or "earn" such treatment, but everyone in the Mediterranean world of antiquity and the present seeks to have a patron.

The vineyard owner treats the last hired generously and graciously, "as if" they were relatives. They did nothing to "earn" such treatment. The owner gave them "what is right" for relatives. At the same time, the owner treats the first hired in accord with their agreement. If he chose to, the owner could disregard the agreement and treat the first hired generously, "as if" they were relatives. But he doesn't so choose. To the first hired, the vineyard owner chooses to be employer; to the last hired, the vineyard owner chooses to be a patron.

"IS YOUR EYE EVIL?"

The frustrated first-hired workers come to a shocking awareness: they are nothing more than "hired hands." How can they get even with the owner? By casting an "evil-eye" on the owner's wealth! In many English translations, the phrase "Are you envious" (v. 15) replaces the literal Greek, "Is your eye evil?" "Envy" is a good translation provided one fully appreciates the Middle Eastern understanding of envy. It is not simply a desire for something another person has (e.g., a vineyard like his), but a desire for exactly that item (e.g., that very vineyard). Such a desire involves a wish for the death of the owner or, failing that, a wish for the utter destruction of that vineyard. In either case, the envious person hopes that the owner of the object envied will actually lose it.

Jesus' lesson is not about economics but about God from a Middle Eastern perspective. Insinuated in Jesus' explanation is that God's choice for treating people may reflect how people deal with God. Such ideas clash with American economic ideas of equal opportunity, contracts, seniority, and the like. How should God behave from an American perspective?

Twenty-Sixth Sunday in Ordinary Time
Matthew 21:28-32

A Christian missionary in the Middle East used to share this parable about the two sons (only verses 28-30) with villagers that he visited and ask: "Which was the better son?" The vast majority answered that the son who said yes to his father even though he did not go to work in the vineyard was without doubt the better son. The son's reply was honorable and respectful. It was what the father wanted to hear. That he never went to work in the vineyard is beside the point, which in the Middle East is always honor.

Remember that life in the Middle East is very public. Honor, the core value of this culture, requires such publicity. The dialogue between the father and his sons in this parable takes place not in private, just between two at a time, but rather in public, within view and earshot of many villagers. Like their modern-day descendants, the Middle Eastern villagers in this parable favor the respectful but disobedient son over the disrespectful but obedient son.

THE IDEAL AND THE REAL

All cultures distinguish between the ideal and reality, but the gap between these two is greater in other cultures than in the ancient Middle East, generally speaking. Westerners generally believe that the ideal is the norm by which reality should be judged. If reality does not measure up to the ideal, it is flawed.

Some Middle Eastern cultures prefer to blur the line between the ideal and the real. Like modern Middle Eastern respondents to Jesus' parable, the ancients too would believe–against reality–that giving an honorable answer is enough. In their mind, conforming to the ideal of speaking respectfully is sufficient to fulfill the commandment to *"honor* one's father [and mother]" (Deut 5:16).

Honor is a public claim to worth that is confirmed by public acknowledgement of that claim by others. The father gives a very public command to two sons. His claim to honor is that the sons will respond with respect. The public watches the responses. One son responds honorably, and in the judgment of the crowd the father's claim is valid and affirmed. The other son responds shamefully, he publicly humiliates his father, and the crowd's immediate judgment would deny the father's claim to honor in this instance. It is not likely that the crowd or the father went to check on the subsequent behavior of each son.

JESUS' CHALLENGE

Jesus did not ask which son behaved honorably. He asked: "Which of the two *did the will* of his father?" (v. 31). Modern Middle Easterners would certainly echo the judgment of Jesus' listeners: "The first," that is, the one who ultimately went and worked in the vineyard as he was directed by his father. They recognized the importance of obedience, but the honorable appearance was more important.

THE EXPLANATION

Jesus addressed this parable to the chief priests and elders (v. 23) who approached him while he taught in the Temple and asked for his credentials: "By what authority are you doing these things, and who gave you this authority?" "We, the legitimate Temple authorities, didn't commission or license you." They challenge Jesus' honor.

The parable of the two sons serves Jesus as a master strategy for defending his honor and presenting a counter-challenge to his adversaries. The point of the parable was quite clear to the listeners. With his explanation, Jesus rubs salt into the wound his parable has opened. The toll collectors and harlots are like the first son. Initially they said no to God, but hearing John the Baptist's preaching they converted and are doing what pleases God. The chief priests and elders are like the second son. They too heard John's preaching and saw the responses of the toll collectors and harlots. They feigned acceptance but refused to accept John as a messenger from God. They gave an honorable word, but that is not enough. "Not everyone who says to me, 'Lord, Lord,' will enter the reign of God, but only the one who does the will of my Father in heaven" (Matt 7:21). Is this what Americans mean when they identify some religious people as hypocrites?

Twenty-Seventh Sunday in Ordinary Time
Matthew 21:33-43

Today's parable offers an opportunity to appreciate the complexity of the gospel tradition. Matthew's version of the parable contains elements that are difficult to attribute to Jesus: allusions to the Greek Bible (vv. 33, 42), allegorical features (the vineyard is Israel, the tenant farmers are Israel's leaders, the householder is God, etc.), and others.

The version of this parable in the Coptic (= the Egyptian tradition) *Gospel of Thomas* 65 (dating from the beginning of the third century) doesn't contain allegorical elements and may be closer to the parable Jesus originally spoke. In this simpler form, the parable reflects a reality familiar to all peasants, namely, the extortion practiced by hard-nosed absentee landowners.

A SIMPLE PARABLE

The vineyard owner lives in a different country (v. 33). This was a common experience among peasants in Galilee. The owner rented the vineyard out to tenant farmers or sharecroppers who worked the land in return for a fee or a percentage of the crop. The owner sent his agents on a regular basis to collect what was due.

Modern scholars have pieced together bits and pieces of information to gain a better understanding of the situation of tenant farmers based on what is known about peasant freeholders, that is, peasants who were fortunate enough to own and farm their own land. Some of the crop would have to be used for trade to gain other necessities of life. There were also social dues (gifts), religious tithes, and taxes adding up to about 35 or 40 percent. About 20 percent of the annual produce would be left to feed the family and livestock of a freeholding peasant. Far less would be left to tenant farmers who also owed land rent.

From this perspective, the parable is easy to interpret. The tenant farmers are frustrated, desperate, and driven to violence. They beat and kill the first two delegations from the owner. When the owner's son shows up, they miscalculate and presume that the owner is dead. Believing the son to be the sole surviving heir, they kill him in hope of gaining the vineyard for themselves. The plan is stupid and illegal, but they are driven by their otherwise hopeless situation. The owner is very much alive. Everyone knows what his response will be. He will avenge himself against these foolish tenant farmers and lease to more compliant tenants. The owner will not be deprived or defrauded of his harvest. If this was the form of the parable Jesus told, it was a warning to landowners against selfishly hoarding their harvest or exporting it.

AN ALLEGORIZED PARABLE

In general, a parable makes one point. The story is about an absentee landlord and his tenant farmers. In an allegory, every element of the story means something else. Good storytellers don't explain their stories (or jokes). The point is clear. When a story or parable is interpreted, inevitably the meaning is not what appears on the surface.

In verse 43 Jesus (or the preachers, or Matthew) appears to make an allegory out of the parable, perhaps on the basis of Isaiah 5:1-7. But note carefully the differences between Matthew and Isaiah. There are no tenant farmers in Isaiah; God destroyed the vineyard itself. In Matthew, the tenant farmers are destroyed, and the vineyard given to others. The chief priests and Pharisees (v. 45) realize the parable is directed against them and would arrest Jesus were it not for Jesus' popularity with the crowds, who regard him as a prophet.

Clearly in Matthew the problem lies with the leadership of Israel and not with Israel itself as in Isaiah (5:5-6). The tenant farmers, that is, the leadership, must be replaced because they have not born fruit (see Matt 3:8, 10; 7:16-20; 12:33; 13:8; 21:19). Thus, leadership will be transferred from the present group which has failed to a different group (preferable to the word "people" in v. 43) that will produce proper fruit. This group is best identified as the leaders of the Judean-Christian community.

The simple parable raises probing questions about the responsibilities of land ownership and relationships with tenants or workers. Matthew's allegorized parable urges his contemporaries and modern-day Christians and Jews (and all people of different creeds) to reflect upon mutual relationships. It does not support any idea that one people is superior to or will replace another.

Twenty-Eighth Sunday in Ordinary Time
Matthew 22:1-14

Some background knowledge of meals in antiquity sheds light on today's parable. Meals reproduce in miniature the everyday social relations of a society. Who eats with whom at a given table reflects who can associate with whom in the larger society.

THE INSULTS OF THE FIRST GROUP

In today's story, a king is arranging a wedding banquet for his son. In any society, commoners will not likely be invited. Royalty associate almost exclusively with royalty or at least with VIPs. Among the king's invited guests are a landowner and a business person (v. 5), definitely members of the elite class.

Notice also the double invitation: "The king sent his slaves *to call those who had been invited. . . .* Again he sent other slaves, saying . . . 'Come!'" (vv. 3-5). This was a common practice in antiquity. After the first invitation, the guests checked out who was invited or not invited, what kind of preparations were being made or not being made, and who was planning to attend as well as who was planning to stay away. This last point was particularly important. If key people decided to stay away, so would others.

The refusal of the invited guests to attend the king's wedding party shames him. For some reason the guests disapproved of the arrangements the king was making. They offer flimsy and insulting excuses, implying that tending the farm or the business is much more important than the wedding of the king's son. This is the traditional and indirect or face-saving method of turning down an invitation.

Other invited guests challenge the king's honor in a more direct fashion. They seize his slaves who bring the invitation, beat, and kill them. Clearly this action demands redress, and the king obliges (see v. 7).

First, he sends troops to kill the murderers and burn their city. This evens the score and solidifies the king's honor according to the rules of the honor and shame game. But then the king does something that breaks the rules. He invites nonelites to the wedding feast. Going to the palace, these people will enter a section of the city where they are rarely, if ever, seen.

UNEXPECTED INVITATIONS

The word in verse 9 translated as "main roads, main streets, or thoroughfares" actually describes the squares or plazas into which the streets run. These open spaces are common in Mediterranean cities. They are the normal places where the elite might meet and communicate with the nonelite. It is the place to see and be seen.

The king's guest list now is very unusual to say the least. In antiquity, meals were an exclusive affair. Inclusive table fellowship in the early Christian community caused problems, as Paul noted in his letters to Corinth (e.g., 1 Cor 11:17-34). People in a status-conscious culture such as this would feel more than uneasy with the royal banquet.

But more than this, the king has taken a bold and risky step. Bringing nonelites to his table to eat with him could prompt his fellow elites to cut all ties with him. Worse, any elite person who had already determined to attend the king's wedding feast would face the same consequences as the king. Since all of life and survival itself in the Mediterranean world depends on one's social network, for an elite to eat with nonelite would be the equivalent of suicide.

Yet even among this second group of guests, someone refused to put on the garment provided by the king for the occasion. We do not know why, but this guest decides to shame and insult the king. The king has no choice but to shame the guest instead and have him ejected from the feast.

Jesus' parable was directed against his elite opponents from Jerusalem, the chief priests and elders. He contrasts their rigid observance of exclusivity with the open-hearted inclusivity expressed by the king: "Invite everyone you find" in the city square. Remember, parables tell how God relates to his clients ("the reign of God is like . . ."). The implication is that God's people ought to relate to each other in the same way. Do we?

Twenty-Ninth Sunday in Ordinary Time
Matthew 22:15-21

In ancient Mediterranean culture, no question is neutral. It is always intended and perceived as a challenge to one's honor. Today's gospel portrays Jesus once again as a master of the cultural game of challenge and riposte.

SETTING THE TRAP

So far Jesus has been fencing with the chief priests and elders. Now the Pharisees and Herodians launch an attack on him. Matthew's editorial comment leaves no doubt about their intentions: the Pharisees intend to entrap Jesus by what he says (22:15). They enlist the Herodians in their plot.

The questioners begin with flattery to take Jesus off guard. A Pharisee compliments Jesus on being "honest" (true, a truthful man), teaching the way of God authentically, and caring little about honor, that is, taking no account of any person's status or opinion. In actuality, Jesus was very sensitive to honor. He did care about the opinions of others (Matt 16:13). Eagerness to trap Jesus causes the Pharisees to exaggerate. Jesus is not taken in.

The question too is flattering. It acknowledges that Jesus is qualified to explain the Torah. "Does it accord with the Torah to pay taxes to the emperor or not?" The specific tax here is a head or poll tax required of every man, woman, and slave between the ages of twelve and sixty-five. It amounted to a denarius, that is, a day's wages. This was the price of living in and enjoying rights as a subject of the Roman Empire.

Jesus was aware of the malice behind the question and understood the challenge. If he said it was not lawful to pay the tax, he would anger the Roman officials. If he said it was in accord with Torah, he would offend the ardent nationalists who hated everything about the Romans.

TURNING THE TABLES

"Show me the coin that pays the census tax," says Jesus. Before they recognize Jesus' trap, they produce the specific coin. In the time of Jesus, the denarius bore the image of the emperor Tiberius, who ruled between 14 and 37 C.E., and an inscription: "Tiberius Caesar, Augustus, son of the divine Augustus, high priest."

Pharisees were particularly disturbed by the attribution of divinity to Caesar but also considered possession of this graven image to be idolatrous. They devised ways to pay this tax without possessing or handling the coin. It would be very shameful if a Pharisee produced the coin. But if a Herodian in the group produced the coin, the Pharisees would still be shamed by having selected unworthy allies. In either case, the fact that someone in their group possessed and produced the coin was shameful. Jesus' first riposte to their challenge cuts deep.

His second riposte lies in his questions: "Whose head? Whose title?" The inscription and image were plainly visible and clearly legible. The Pharisees' reply sets up Jesus' positive answer: "Repay to Caesar what belongs to Caesar." Later (see Luke 23:2) the Pharisees will lie and say that Jesus answered negatively.

Actually, Jesus and the Pharisees probably held similar opinions about paying the tax. It could cause more trouble not to pay it. Life is preferable to death, and if this is what it costs to coexist peaceably with the Romans in their empire, so be it.

WHAT REALLY MATTERS

Jesus' concluding exhortation, "Give to God the things that belong to God," implies that neither the Pharisees nor the Herodians are doing that. This is a serious charge. The Pharisees were so devoted to observing the Torah's 613 commandments that they put a "hedge around the Torah." They proposed observing just a little bit more to be sure of pleasing God. Was Jesus exaggerating their minor foibles as the Pharisees earlier exaggerated Jesus' insensitivity to honor? Whatever the case, Jesus won this contest and reminded his adversaries that what mattered most was pleasing God.

Americans tend to see in this passage an argument for the separation of church and state. Such an idea makes no sense in first-century Mediterranean culture. Religion and economics both are embedded in politics and kinship. There was state religion (Temple; empire) and family religion (home); state economics (taxes and redistribution) and family economics (gifts and sharing). Our modern Western situation and its challenges are very different. For us as for our ancestors what matters most is to please God.

Thirtieth Sunday in Ordinary Time
Matthew 22:34-40

Jesus' statement on the greatest commandment is probably the best-known and most-discussed passage in all of Scripture. Placed in its Mediterranean cultural context, it takes on a fresh and concrete meaning.

The episode is yet another example of the continuous cultural game of challenge and riposte. The text clearly states that the Pharisee intends his question as a challenge ("to test him," v. 34). (The Greek manuscript evidence for "lawyer" is not very strong. It was probably inserted here due to influence from Luke 10:25.)

THE RELATIVE IMPORTANCE OF THE COMMANDMENTS

On the face of it, the question appears very honest. The Pharisees identified 613 commandments in the Torah (the first five books of the Bible). Two hundred forty-eight were positive ("thou shalt") and three hundred sixty-five were negative ("thou shalt not"). How could anyone remember all of them? Were some more important than others?

Some teachers distinguished between "heavy" and "light" commandments. The "Ten" (e.g., honor father and mother) are examples of heavy or serious commandments. An example of a light or less serious commandment is Deuteronomy 22:6-7, which stipulates that a person who finds a bird's nest with a mother sitting on eggs or with young may take the young but must let the mother go. The reason for observing both is "that it may go well with you, and that you may live long" (Deut 5:16; 22:7).

Another custom was to sum up the Torah's commandments in a small number of precepts or a summary statement. Thus King David proposed eleven (Ps 15), Isaiah six (33:15), Micah three (6:8), and Amos only one (5:4).

Jesus once prescribed: "In everything do to others as you would have them do to you; for this is the law and the prophets" (Matt 7:12). It sounds very similar to something said by the great Jewish teacher Hillel, who may still have been alive when Jesus was born: "What is hateful to you do not do to your neighbor; that is the whole Torah, while the rest is commentary on it; go and learn it" (Babylonian Talmud, Sabb. 31a).

In reply to the Pharisee's question about the "greatest commandment," Jesus combines two: "Love the Lord your God with all your heart, and with all your soul, and with all your mind" (citing and amending Deut 6:5). And the second of equal importance is "love your neighbor as yourself" (citing Lev 19:18). Jesus does not discard other commandments. He explicitly adds: "On these two commandments hang *all* the law and the prophets."

Essentially, Jesus' answer is very orthodox, very traditional. If there is any distinctiveness, it lies in his understanding of neighbor which he explains in Luke 10:29-33 but not at this point. (Leviticus specifies neighbor as brother, that is, fellow Israelite. Luke's Jesus expands the concept of neighbor to be more inclusive.)

LOVE

More importantly, what does Jesus understand by love? Mediterranean cultural anthropology sheds some light. Remember that our ancestors in the faith were strongly group centered. The group was family, village, neighborhood, and factions (like the Twelve, the Pharisees, etc.) which a person might join.

The group gave a sense of identity, a sense of belonging, and advice for actions to be taken or avoided. The group was an external conscience exerting enormous pressure on its individual members.

In this context, love and hate are best understood as group attachment and group disattachment. Whether emotion or affection is involved is beside the point. The major feeling in love and hate is a feeling of belonging or not belonging, respectively. Thus, to love God with all one's heart is to be totally attached to God. To love neighbor as self is to be as totally attached to people in one's neighborhood or immediate circle of friends (i.e., fellow Israelites) as one is to one's family group. This has been and continues to be the normal way of life in the Mediterranean world, unless feuding develops.

To "hate one's father, mother," and others as Luke's Jesus (14:26) requires of his followers means to detach oneself from family and join the Jesus group. Paul says the greatest among the virtues faith, hope, and charity is charity, that is, love or attachment to the group. The group-attachment aspect of love poses a challenge to individualistically oriented, emotional American believers. Which commandment would American believers say is the greatest? And what does that mean?

Thirty-First Sunday in Ordinary Time
Matthew 23:1-12

Too much of a good thing is never beneficial. Here, Jesus shows himself to be a master of insult, a skill deliberately honed and widely admired in his culture. But the intensity and quantity of insults heaped up highlights serious disagreement between Jesus and his adversaries, the scribes and the Pharisees.

The introduction of these adversaries to replace the "chief priests and elders" with whom Jesus had been jousting until now suggests to some scholars that this episode reflects conditions in Matthew's community some fifty years after Jesus died. With the destruction of the Temple in 70 C.E., chief priests and elders lost status as authorities in the community.

Matthew's Jesus has three objections: the Pharisaic scribes do not practice what they preach, they adopt a very narrow and burdensome interpretation of the Torah, and they seek public acknowledgment.

PRACTICE WHAT YOU PREACH

Jesus' exhortation to do what the Pharisaic scribes teach is a compliment to their expertise. They know the Scripture and interpret it well. Sadly, Scripture is not the script by which they live. This is why Jesus calls them "actors" (the literal translation of the Greek word usually rendered "hypocrites," a word Matthew's Jesus uses repeatedly when talking about the Pharisees). Jesus discourages imitating these actors.

STRICT INTERPRETATION

Recall that some Pharisaic scribes distinguished "heavy" or serious commandments and "light" or less serious commandments among the 613 they identified in the Torah, while others did not. In Jesus' day, each approach was represented by a famous teacher and expert in the Torah. Hillel typically favored a broad interpretation, while Shammai typically favored a strict or narrow interpretation. Strict interpreters laid heavy burdens on others and refused to lighten the burdens by means of a broader interpretation of obligation (see v. 4).

EXCESSIVE STATUS SEEKING

Everyone in this culture needs to be seen and affirmed publicly in order to have status or honor. Jesus' complaint therefore concerns excess in the search for recognition and acclaim. Imagine the excess that must have characterized the Pharisees' phylacteries and cloak fringes if Jesus' charge is to make sense to his listeners. One can almost hear an appreciative burst of laughter from the crowd.

The same is true of the Pharisees' desire for honorable places and titles. Mediterranean culture requires of all a measure of humility. One is taught from youth to stay at least one step behind one's rightful status: "Do not sit in a place of honor" (Luke 14:8). This insures against trespassing upon someone else's right (a more eminent person will displace you, Luke 14:8-9) and gives others the opportunity to grant you the honor and title you deserve ("Friend, go higher," Luke 14:10).

In discouraging grasping after titles, Jesus mentions "rabbi," "father," and "teacher" or director, moral guide, guru. "Rabbi," which means "my Lord," was simply a title of honor in the first century. In verse 8, "rabbi" seems to mean teacher. The modern meaning and role of rabbi did not begin to emerge and develop until the third century C.E., and only in contemporary America did rabbis come to be considered clergy.

In the first century, the term "father" was applied to elders (see *Sayings of the Fathers*, 2.10-12) and certain respected deceased persons. Matthew uses the title only of God. Jesus taught his followers to address God as Father (Matt 6:9). The point quite simply is that Jesus' disciples ought not to engage in an all-consuming search for honor by selecting titles, like "father," that they may not deserve. This passage has no relationship at all to the modern practice of addressing ordained male priests with the title "father."

We know that leaders in Matthew's community considered themselves to be the counterparts to the Pharisaic scribes who were leaders in Judean communities. What is implied in each of Jesus' statements is that Christian leaders are exactly the opposite: they practice what they preach, follow Jesus in lightening the yoke of the Torah (see Matt 11:28-30), seek to forego claims to honor from other human beings (see Matt 6:1, 3, 6, 18), and prefer lower status and service to lording it over others.

How do American believers practice what they preach, apply restrictive laws benignly, and strive for humility?

Thirty-Second Sunday in Ordinary Time
Matthew 25:1-13

MEDITERRANEAN WEDDINGS

How does God behave toward us? "The reign of God" is like a first-century Mediterranean wedding (see comments on the Fourth Sunday of Advent). In this period of Israel's history, families practiced what is known as *patrilocal* marriage. The bride moved to the groom's home which would have been located in or close to the home of his father.

Anyone who has visited Peter's house in Capernaum or seen reconstructions of the house plan recalls that a cluster of homes formed a complex in which Jonah and his wife and children, single and married, all lived. This included Peter, his wife and children (and mother-in-law), and his brother Andrew.

The ideal marriage partner in this culture is a first cousin, specifically, a father's brother's daughter (or son as the case may require). If Peter married his first cousin, then his mother-in-law was also his aunt. Middle Eastern families of antiquity and the present are close-knit units, and these wedding practices explain why.

Contemporary Westerners wonder whether the children of these marriages were healthy. Our culture forbids such marriages because of the supposed risk of birth defects and mental deficiencies. Contemporary scientific research, however, indicates that the incidence of mental retardation or other birth defects traditionally associated with marrying close relatives is no higher in that culture than in ours.

The marriage was arranged by the fathers under the powerful influence of the mothers; it was ratified with a contract negotiated between the mothers but signed ultimately by the patriarch. The purpose of such a marriage was to join two families. When the partners were old enough, the long marriage ceremony was celebrated. The highpoint of the ceremony occurred when the groom, accompanied by his relatives, went to the family house of the bride to transfer her to his home. It is here that the rest of the wedding ceremony and celebration took place.

THE TEN TEENAGERS

This is the point at which Jesus begins his parable. The groom has gone to fetch his bride. Ten young teenagers, very likely the groom's sisters and cousins, are awaiting his return. ("Bridesmaids" is not a good translation.) Five are clever and five are dull-witted.

The role of the teenagers in the ceremony is to greet the groom and the entire wedding party when it returns and to participate in the celebration as everyone waits for the consummation of the marriage and the display of the blood-stained bed sheet to demonstrate that the bride possessed physical integrity as required by Deuteronomy 22:13-21.

The clever teenagers were prepared for their roles, but the dull-witted failed to make adequate plans and found themselves shut out of the feast. They didn't even know how to put the bridegroom's delay to advantage.

As with all parables, so too does this one have a double meaning: it is about a wedding party but also about something else, namely about how God relates to human beings.

DEPENDENCE ON THE PATRON

The image of God behind all the gospel parables is based on the Mediterranean institution called patronage. Each of us has a human father, but God is perceived by Middle Easterners as a father in the sense of a patron, a "godfather." A patron or godfather treats select people "as if" they were family members. Middle Eastern people consider themselves very fortunate when someone chooses to be their patron. They do their best not to lose that privileged position but rather to strengthen it with the passage of time. Thus, they must be very clever, ever sensitive to the patron's whims, fancies, and wishes. Dull-witted clients risk losing their privileged position, just like the dull-witted teenagers in the parable. The moral: strive to be clever in your relationship with God.

After Jesus' death and resurrection, Christians awaiting his imminent return added verse 13 to his parable: "So keep awake, for you know neither the day nor the hour." It ill fits the parable. All ten young teens fell asleep (25:5)! But it is good advice if one is thinking about the return of Jesus or the end of the world. The parable provides both positive and negative models. Which will you follow?

Thirty-Third Sunday in Ordinary Time
Matthew 25:14-30

This parable explaining how the rich get richer follows quite naturally upon the rewards of being a clever teenage participant in a wedding celebration (Matt 25:1-13). But note well that the parable does not begin with the usual: "The reign of God is like. . . ." As we review the text, ask yourself if this indeed is how you would like God to behave toward human beings.

THE PROBLEMS OF WEALTH

A very rich person about to set off on a journey entrusted very large sums of wealth to three slaves, each according to his personal ability. In no time at all, the first two slaves doubled their trust. The third slave buried his trust in the ground.

On the day of accounting, the master applauds and rewards the two clever slaves but punishes the third slave whom he calls "wicked and slothful" (v. 26). He takes the third slave's trust and gives it to the first slave.

This parable is a favorite with American capitalists (interested in profit) and fundamentalist guidance counselors (focusing on the unintended and textually unsupported meaning of the word *talent*). Jesus' listeners, of course, were neither capitalists nor committed to self-improvement. They were peasants. Would these interpretations bring good news to a peasant?

In first-century Mediterranean culture people believed that all goods already exist and are already distributed. There is no more where this came from, and the only way to get more is to defraud another. Anyone who suddenly acquired something "more" was automatically judged to be a thief. Wealthy people were especially under suspicion. How could they honorably increase their wealth? They commissioned slaves to handle their affairs. Everyone knew slaves were shameless, and dishonorable behavior was all one could expect from them.

A GREEDY MASTER

The very rich man in this story sounds like an honorable person at the outset. It is only at the conclusion that we learn that he is dishonorable. As the third slave states, the very rich master is "a hard man," reaping what he did not sow and gathering where he did not scatter seed (v. 24). Putting a good face on his behavior, we modern Westerners would call him a clever, industrious, and enterprising entrepreneur. Others, like our Middle Eastern ancestors in the faith, would call him arrogant, opportunistic, greedy, and rapacious. The master agrees with the slave's description of him(!); (see v. 26) and confirms it by saying the slave should at least have put his money in the bank at usury.

Now we understand that the first two slaves did not simply serve their rich master; they imitated him. Why not? If you can't beat the system, join it. Any human being can be as greedy as the next, and joining forces with a ruthless and unconscionable but successful master gives one a leg up on others like that pitiful third slave.

Actually, the third slave did what the rabbis would later commend as the safest and therefore most honorable course of action *for a freeman.* But was it proper behavior for a slave?

ALTERNATIVE MEANINGS

A peasant audience hearing Jesus' parable and reflecting on their own life wouldn't find this good news at all. The rich get richer, and we continue to be abused (see v. 29). If God behaves no better than the rich master, who needs God?

The church historian Eusebius saw the problem in Matthew's text quite clearly and reported a different version of this same parable familiar to him in the Gospel of the Nazoreans (now lost). In this version, the master throws the first slave into prison, scolds the second slave, but welcomes the honorable third slave with joy. Was this the version Jesus told?

Matthew's version offers advice to his community around the year 80 C.E. about how to behave in the period after Jesus' resurrection and ascension while they await his imminent second coming. They should not be lazy and worthless but rather should imitate the cleverness but not the greed of their masters. In other words, when it comes to the kingdom, the risk of cleverness is preferable to the numbing security of doing the proper and honorable thing, or "playing it safe." Jesus' own life manifested similar risky choices.

Believers who can suspend their view of this parable as presenting strategies for fund raising or developing personal abilities and adopt instead the peasant view will have much to think about.

Thirty-Fourth Sunday in Ordinary Time (Christ the King)
Matthew 25:31-46

Identifying the Middle Eastern cultural elements of this familiar scene help place it in an unfamiliar focus.

HONOR AND SHAME

First notice the explicit and very pointed context of honor and shame, the core values of Mediterranean culture. The Son of Man comes "in glory" (= honor) and sits on the "throne of his glory" (= honor). All his angels accompany him (= honor) and all the nations will witness the scene (= honor). The king (vv. 33 and 40, same as the Son of Man) separates honorable people from dishonorable people as a shepherd separates sheep (= honor) from goats (= shame).

SHEEP AND GOATS

The earliest animals to be domesticated were sheep and goats. They are very common in the Middle East, and the Hebrew language is particularly rich in vocabulary that distinguishes sheep according to sex and age. Our ancestors in the faith were impressed that sheep suffer in silence. They compared men to sheep and considered suffering in silence to be the sign of a real man (Isa 53:7; Acts 8:32-35; Mark 15:25-37). Sheep came to symbolize honor, virility, and strength.

Goats were considered lascivious animals. Unlike rams (male sheep), goats allow other males access to their females. A man whose wife was ravished by another man was (and in the Middle East still is) considered like a goat. Goats symbolize shame and shameful behavior. The ram was associated with honorable Greek gods like Zeus, Apollo, and Poseidon, while the goat was associated with Greek gods known for shameful and unrestrained behavior like Pan, Bacchus, and Aphrodite. Goats also are associated with women (women keep goats and milk them) and the devil (see Matt 25:33, 41).

INGROUP AND OUTGROUP

The separation of sheep and goats is a symbolic way of drawing even stronger lines between an ingroup (sheep) and an outgroup (goats). Matthew's Jesus sent his disciples only to the "lost sheep of the house of Israel" (the ingroup) and were forbidden from going "among the Gentiles" or entering any "town of the Samaritans" (outgroups, see Matt 10:5).

An ingroup generally consists of one's household and one's extended family and friends. People from the same village are ingroup when they meet elsewhere, but in the village they may belong to one of the outgroups. The boundaries are fluid.

Outsiders looking at Israel saw a single ingroup and called them Judeans (in Greek, *Ioudaioi,* a term sometimes erroneously translated and interpreted as "Jews"). Israel, the single ingroup, tended to consider all the rest of the world as one large outgroup. There are references to "all [the other] nations" (Matt 25:32) or "the Gentiles" (Matt 10:5).

HOSPITALITY

What is the basis for this final, definite determination of ingroup (sheep) and outgroup (goats)? Hospitality! In the Middle East, hospitality is extended mainly by men and solely to complete strangers. (Kindness extended to relatives is not hospitality but steadfast love, a very frequent term in the Old Testament describing what God offers to Israel.)

The "sheep" extended hospitality to strangers ("Lord, when was it that we saw you hungry, etc.?" v. 37-40); the "goats" neglected that opportunity (vv. 44-45; compare Matt 10:40).

APPLICATION

One traditional interpretation of this episode makes it a judgment scene involving all humanity ("all the nations") and all people in poverty, need, and distress ("the least"). This view is popular with preachers and social activists. But Jesuit biblical scholar Daniel Harrington argues that the judgment concerns how "all the Gentiles" (instead of "nations") treated Christians or Christian missionaries, "these least brothers of mine" (Matt 25:40, 45).

The treatment should have been hospitable, in the Middle Eastern understanding. This same hospitality was earlier expected from the "lost sheep of the house of Israel" toward Christian missionaries (Matt 10:5). It was on this basis that the missionaries would know whether to stay and evangelize or move on.

Ultimately, in the Middle Eastern view, it boils down to a matter of honor. Any Middle Easterner–Israelite, Christian, pagan–is expected to treat strangers hospitably. Whoever does so has treated Jesus hospitably and will enjoy companionship with God in the kingdom. How can a contemporary believer translate this into American culture where honor does not count for very much (except in the military academies)?

Recommended Readings

Dunning, James B. *Echoing God's Word.* Arlington, Va: The North American Forum on the Catechumenate, 1992.

Elliott, John H. "Matthew 20:1-15: A Parable of Invidious Comparison and Evil Eye Accusation." *Biblical Theology Bulletin* 22 (1992) 52–65.

Harrington, Daniel J., S.J. *The Gospel of Matthew.* Sacra Pagina 1. Collegeville: The Liturgical Press, 1991.

Malina, Bruce J. *Windows on the World of Jesus: Time Travel to Ancient Judea.* Louisville: Westminster/John Knox Press, 1993.

———. "What is Prayer?" *The Bible Today* 18 (1980) 214–220.

Malina, Bruce J., and Richard L. Rohrbaugh. *Social-Science Commentary on the Synoptic Gospels.* Minneapolis: Fortress, 1992.

McKay, Heather A. "From Evidence to Edifice: Four Fallacies about the Sabbath." In *Text as Pretext: Essays in Honour of Robert Davidson,* ed. Robert P. Carroll. Sheffield: JSOT Press, 1992. Pp. 179–199.

Neyrey, Jerome H., S.J. "What's Wrong With This Picture? John 4, Cultural Stereotypes of Women, and Public and Private Space." *Biblical Theology Bulletin* 24 (1994) 77–91.

———. *The Resurrection Stories.* Zacchaeus Studies: New Testament. Collegeville: The Liturgical Press, A Michael Glazier Book, 1988.

Pilch, John J. "The Transfiguration of Jesus: An Experience of Alternate Reality." In *Modelling Early Christianity,* ed. Philip F. Esler. London: Routledge, 1995.

_____. "Illuminating the World of Jesus through Cultural Anthropology." *The Living Light* 31 (1994) 20–31.

_____. *The Triduum: Breaking Open the Scriptures of Holy Week.* Columbus: Initiatives Publications, 1993.

_____. *Introducing the Cultural Context of the New Testament.* Hear the Word! Volume 2. New York and Mahwah: Paulist Press, 1991.

_____. "Praying with Luke." *The Bible Today* 18 (1980) 221–225.

Pilch, John J., and Bruce J. Malina, eds. *Biblical Social Values and the Meaning: A Handbook.* Peabody, Mass.: Hendrickson, 1993.

Rohrbaugh, Richard L. "A Peasant Reading of the Parable of the Talents/Pounds: A Text of Terror?" *Biblical Theology Bulletin* 23 (1993) 32–39.